# Separation of Church and State

Jonathan A. Wright

Historical Guides to Controversial Issues in America

 GREENWOOD

AN IMPRINT OF ABC-CLIO, LLC
Santa Barbara, California • Denver, Colorado • Oxford, England

**Library of Congress Cataloging-in-Publication Data**

Wright, Jonathan A.
  Separation of church and state / Jonathan A. Wright.
    p. cm. — (Historical guides to controversial issues in America)
  Includes bibliographical references and index.
    ISBN 978-0-313-34769-6 (hardcopy : alk. paper) —
ISBN 978-0-313-34770-2 (ebook)   1. Church and state—United States—
History.   2. United States—Religion.   3. United States—Social
conditions.   4. United States—Politics and government.   I. Title.
  BR516.W75   2010
  261.7—dc22        2010009531

ISBN: 978-0-313-34769-6
EISBN: 978-0-313-34770-2

14 13 12 11 10   1 2 3 4 5

This book is also available on the World Wide Web as an eBook.
Visit www.abc-clio.com for details.

Greenwood
An Imprint of ABC-CLIO, LLC

ABC-CLIO, LLC
130 Cremona Drive, P.O. Box 1911
Santa Barbara, California 93116-1911

This book is printed on acid-free paper ∞

Manufactured in the United States of America.

# Contents

# Introduction

Few issues in American history have generated quite so much controversy as the relationship between Church and State. For four hundred years, from the earliest colonial days to the Supreme Court decisions of the 20th and early 21st centuries, quarrels about the interaction between the secular and religious realms have raged. They show little sign of abating. This centuries-long process has sometimes provided clarification, but as often as not, it has muddied the waters. The fact that the United States still seems unable to reach definitive conclusions about the Church–State conundrum just goes to show how contentious that issue is and always has been.

This book provides a whistle-stop tour through America's encounter with this most puzzling of topics. It is aimed at the general reader, and so, for the most part, it revisits well-trodden historical terrain—the most famous incidents and personalities in this long and winding story. It also adopts the broadest possible historical perspective. In recent times there has sometimes been a tendency, on both sides of a furious debate, to glibly recruit ideas and individuals from bygone eras in order to shore up current-day arguments. This is a regrettable, often misleading, and from the historian's point of view, rather disreputable tendency. We should always remember that our conception of Church–State relations is very much the product of its time.

Avoiding anachronism or unnecessary generalization is therefore vitally important. Americans of the 17th century, for instance, would simply not have framed their arguments as we do today. Latter-day, philosophically motivated defenses of religious freedom and pluralism, or of a sharp distinction between sacred and profane concerns, did not enjoy wide cultural currency during this earlier era. This does not make such ideas any less important for our present and continuing purposes: in many ways, they represent the dominant and very welcome pulse-beat of current discourses. It is important to realize, however, that earlier generations often approached the collision between religion and politics in strikingly different ways.

In fact, many of our forebears simply didn't think in terms of a *collision* between the secular and the sacred at all. The notion that, in one way or another, religion ought to shape and influence social and political life was something of a cultural given. Similarly, until the 18th century, it was broadly accepted that one of the politician's chief duties was to support a specific version of Christianity and to play a significant role in striking down any theological challenges that arose. There were some striking exceptions to this rule (and this book will pay them due attention), but the rule was still deeply entrenched in America's social and political worldview. It is worth bearing this in mind, not least because it allows us to produce a more accurate sketch of past religious worlds.

In like fashion, current debates about Church and State are almost always rooted in a discussion of the religious clauses of the First Amendment. This is as it should be in a nation defined by a written constitution, but let us not forget that the men who framed those famous words lived two hundred and more years ago. We are therefore obliged to analyze exactly what they intended and to realize that this was a reflection of the principles and prejudices of their specific historical moment. Deciding how to apply their ideas to the present situation is fraught with difficulty: this is an issue to which we shall return.

Ultimately, when thinking about the history of Church–State relations in America, it makes excellent sense to treat the successive phases of that story on their own historical and decidedly idiosyncratic terms. This is a much wiser approach than constructing reductive, self-serving narratives in which episodes and statements from past eras are plucked out of context in order to score debating points in present-day arguments. Doing so has become a very bad habit in American public life, and this is a cause for considerable lament.

In order to avoid such pitfalls (though it is hard to sidestep them entirely), this book proceeds chronologically. It begins with a short introductory chapter in which we see how a default analysis of Church–State relations emerged in the wake of Constantine's embrace of the Christian faith in the fourth century. At first blush, this might seem long ago and far away, but the notion that, at some basic level, it was the responsibility of a reputable ruler to foster religious orthodoxy—a single vision of Christianity—and to stamp out religious dissent was regnant in western Europe for more than a millennium.

Today, this might strike us as a dubious notion, but crucially, it was the legacy that most of the first American colonists inherited.

Many of those first colonial Americans carried this vision of Church–State relations across the Atlantic Ocean, but during the 17th century, they tinkered and tampered with it in all sorts of intriguing ways. The book explores both the places where older ideas continued, almost unaltered, to hold sway (Virginia, for instance) and the places (Massachusetts being the most conspicuous example) where an obsession with imposing religious uniformity sometimes sat uneasily alongside the radical theology and ecclesiology that defined the New England religious experience. Finally, we visit the colonies, most notably the Rhode Island of Roger Williams and the Pennsylvania of William Penn, where newer ideas about religious freedom and Church–State relations began to emerge.

Next comes the 18th century. In terms of Church–State debates, these were busy decades. First, it became increasingly apparent that a host of young religious denominations—Baptists, Quakers, Methodists, and many more besides—were securing the allegiance of large swathes of the American population. This provoked some very heated arguments, not least courtesy of those who resented the laws and statutes that obliged them to support established state churches to which they owed neither affection nor allegiance. The book explores how two groups—the Baptists in America's northeastern and middle colonies and those of disparate faiths who challenged the Anglican stranglehold in New York—set about voicing their dissent. Also, in the interests of fair play, we will see how members of older, more established faiths sought to meet such challenges.

Two very important trends collided during the 18th century. First, there was the pragmatic realization that, in a nation of so many competing denominations, an insistence on the dominance of a single, state-sponsored variety of Christianity was likely to provoke endless conflict and disaffection. The whole point of imposing a specific version of Christianity (aside from theological concerns) had always been to sustain social and political order and cohesion. It began to dawn on various 18th-century Americans that, in the wake of the fractures and fragmentation of the Reformation (and they showed no sign of dissipating), this older vision had, as it were, run out of steam. In terms of sustaining a peaceable commonwealth, the quest for conformity was likely to do much more harm than good.

Second, largely thanks to the philosophizing of men such as John Locke, a principled belief in the positive value of religious toleration began to gain ground. This was a watershed moment. In fact, it was the cradle of latter-day conceptions of Church–State relations. Such musings came to a head during, and subsequent to, the Revolutionary War, with men such as Thomas

Jefferson, James Madison, and John Leland leading the charge. One of the most enduring consequences of this sea change in attitudes toward Church and State was the First Amendment. At first glance, its religion clauses seemed to offer a neat, coherent summation of how the subject ought to be tackled: "Congress shall make no law respecting an establishment of religion, or prohibiting the free exercise thereof." Interpreting these fabled words proved to be exceptionally difficult, however.

They certainly denied the possibility of a *federally* supported single religious establishment, but during the first decades of the new Republic, there was much debate over whether individual states should still be entitled to privilege (and lavish tax dollars upon) religious denominations. Just as importantly, the Church–State relationship was not simply a matter of legislation. By the middle of the 19th century, it was no longer deemed legitimate for those who wielded political power to actively and purposefully sustain a specific Christian denomination, but this did not mean that the intertwining of politics and religion had become a dead letter. Hardly, if any, of the founding fathers envisaged an America in which Christian ideas would cease to play a formative role in guiding public policy and morality.

It has often been suggested that 19th-century America was still very much a de facto Christian republic—and this almost always meant a *Protestant* republic. This made for a confusing religious environment, especially for non-Protestant Christians, those belonging to the era's many new denominations, and the followers of non-Christian faiths. The letter of the law was often very different from the broader cultural mood, and American attitudes toward Church and State and religious freedom were still very much in flux. The trials and tribulations of minority religious groups (Catholics, Jews, Mormons, and a host of others) and the attempt to curate and interpret the lessons of the First Amendment represent the two key issues confronted by this part of the book.

Finally, we enter the modern era. In the past hundred years, it has become abundantly clear that applying the rubrics of the First Amendment is a very precarious balancing act. Although many have sought to avoid excessive or unnecessary entanglement between Church and State, some have suggested that pursuing this goal too zealously can lead to measures that are openly hostile to religious institutions or those of firm religious faith. Similarly, the amendment suggests that individuals should be allowed to follow the diktats of their consciences, but if a society wants to preserve order, are there not moments when the exercise of religious freedom can threaten social and political stability? What if the free exercise of religion involves the breaking of a secular law? What if the pursuit of religious freedom does damage to the broader well-being of society? It has routinely been argued that, at such times, the state has a compelling interest to intervene and to curtail free exercise.

Sorting out these tricky issues has often been achieved at the local level, out of the media spotlight. Sometimes, though, the debates have made their way into the courtroom. From the 1940s to the present day, the U.S. Supreme Court has confronted dozens of cases in which the specific meaning of the First Amendment's religion clauses have come under the closest scrutiny. The book, without apology, spends much of its time revisiting this post-1940s history. This is where the energy of contemporary debate resides, and it also provides a useful bellwether of developing approaches to the issue.

***

One thing can be stated with certainty. Squabbles about Church and State are still alive and well. The 20th century has seen many non-Christian religious traditions blossom: Islam and Hinduism have gone from strength to strength in America, the beliefs of Native Americans have (belatedly) been accorded due respect, and there are few nations on earth that have produced so many idiosyncratic religious sects and movements. This broadening of the religious landscape is a cause for celebration, but it also has made the issue of Church–State relations even more complicated: the rights of a staggering array of minority faiths (from new branches of Protestantism to those who have cultivated some of the devotional and spiritual ideas carried to America's shores during the era of slavery, to practitioners of Wicca) have come under the judicial microscope. In tandem, the rejection of theism has also scored notable victories, and this too has led to controversy. The First Amendment, by most accounts, was designed to produce an even playing field for those of different faiths: the issue of how those of no faith whatsoever ought to be protected against infringement of their rights has produced more than its share of judicial headaches, and as we shall see, the atheist became a major contributor to debates about Church–State relations from the middle of the 20th century onward.

For all this, were a galaxy-traveling alien to arrive in the United States, he would surely notice that the nation's political and cultural life is still often set against a religious backdrop. "In God We Trust" is still on the currency, children in public schools are obliged to recite a Pledge of Allegiance every morning that talks about their nation being "under God," and presidents still end their speeches with "God bless America." Almost any candidate for high political office is well-advised to attend church services and pay heed to the agendas and petitioning of ministers of varying faiths. The United States has recently enjoyed the most wonderful of watershed moments: the election of its first black president. The election of an avowedly atheistic president remains an unlikely prospect. Whatever the statute book says (and that is still very much a matter of controversy), religion and politics remain very much connected in the popular imagination.

This state of affairs infuriates some Americans. They become even more agitated when new measures and projects are introduced that seem to open up even wider breaches in the fabled wall of separation between Church and State. Recent years have seen heated arguments about voucher programs that give public funds to parents who want to send their children to parochial schools and about faith-based initiatives that provide religious organizations with government-gathered money in order to go about their charitable business. Barely a month goes by without some tussle over prayer in public schools or the rectitude of erecting a Ten Commandments monument or a nativity scene on public property.

Other Americans (some notable Supreme Court justices among them) are convinced that the wall of separation is an unhelpful metaphor: something mentioned in a random letter by Thomas Jefferson (see pp. 62–63) that is in no way an authentic part of the United States' constitutional architecture. Some of them insist that Christian values played a major role in shaping the nation's moral and legal identity and that to forget this is a misguided enterprise. Far from regretting the place of Christian ideals in the broader culture, they suggest that excessive attempts to disentangle Church and State run the risk of obliterating Christianity's crucial role—producing, in the famous phrase, a naked public square.

This is a vibrant, very important debate. There is hyperbole on both sides, and dynamic pressure groups and think tanks clash (sometimes ignorantly) by both day and night. It is an argument that is unlikely to go away. The election of a new member of the Supreme Court still has the ability to provoke forensic investigation of the candidates' attitudes and affiliations. When a school district sets about revising its curriculum, the interested parties inevitably arrive on the scene in order to revisit the burning issue of whether creationism should be taught in a publicly funded science class. Come election time, there are countless tussles over clerics and religious organizations endorsing political candidates.

The Church–State debate has become a whirligig of press releases and legal actions. This can become very confusing and even rather wearisome, not least because the competing positions are so entrenched and unyielding. At the same time, it goes to prove that the issue of Church and State is as vibrant and controversial as ever it was. It shows both the worst and the best of America. On one hand, there is the excessive litigiousness and the often unhelpful partisanship. On the other, there is the enviable commitment to confronting a fascinating, multifaceted political and philosophical question.

In a sense, it would be a shame if concord on the issue of Church–State relations were ever achieved. If this came to pass, a wonderfully enriching debate would be snuffed out. Fortunately, there are few signs that this is going to happen anytime soon. Arguments about how we ought to interpret the First Amendment and understand the relationship between faith and politics look set to continue. On that basis, this short volume hopes to provide you with enough basic historical ammunition to join the debate. Whatever your opinions, it cannot hurt to be historically well informed and respectful of those with whom you disagree. That is the bedrock of sensible, nuanced debate about Church and State, and it is something that America urgently requires.

## ACKNOWLEDGMENTS

I would like to thank the staffs of the British Library, Durham University Library, and Newcastle University Library. Thanks also to my editor, Sandy Towers, and to Angus Wright. The biggest thank you of all goes to Jerome Barker for his dogged enthusiasm.

# 1

# From Constantine to the Reformation: Historical Context

During its first three centuries, Christianity was a much-maligned sect within the Roman Empire. The persecution was neither as persistent nor as systematic as is sometimes supposed, but these were undoubtedly difficult times for the fledgling faith. Under rulers such as Decius and Diocletian, localized efforts to assault Christianity gave way to coordinated, empire-wide attempts at eradication, and Christians from the eastern end of the Mediterranean to the coastal regions of North Africa suffered horribly. Needless to say, there was absolutely no connection between the Christian religion and the Roman state during this period: on the contrary, Christianity was perceived as a subversive and illegal religion. Christian refusal to offer sacrifices to the gods and goddesses of the Roman pantheon was perceived as the most heinous of crimes: a tangible threat to civil and political order.

## THE LEGACY

With the arrival of the emperor Constantine at the beginning of the fourth century, everything changed. Christianity became an accepted faith, and within a few short decades, it had emerged as the legally dominant religion of the empire. This unexpected development was to have momentous consequences for Christianity's future. Suddenly, it became the duty of political rulers to support and sponsor Christianity. Emperors now summoned Church councils and helped to hammer out Christian orthodoxy. They became intimately involved in attacking paganism and heretical variants of Christianity.

This marked the beginning of the long and turbulent relationship between Church and State.

Crucially, largely thanks to the musings of one of the greatest theologians of the early Christian era (Augustine of Hippo), the idea that it was permissible for secular rulers to deploy coercion in order to sustain Christian orthodoxy gathered momentum. Augustine's musings on this issue are often misrepresented—all things being equal, he much preferred persuasion to the use of force, and even *in extremis*, he was uncomfortable with the notion of bodily punishment of heretics—but he certainly helped to inaugurate a new way of confronting heterodoxy. The state was now obliged to intervene, directly and without compromise, in religious affairs.

Christians have long debated whether this was the best or the worst thing that ever happened to their religion. Some have suggested that the arrival of political approval led to a millennium and more of compromise during which the pure Gospel message was sullied by its encounter with worldly authority. Others have pointed out that if Constantine and his successors had not intervened, Christianity might well have dwindled away or, at best, clung on as a minority, illegal sect.

One thing is undeniable: becoming a state-sponsored religion is what allowed Christianity to blossom into a world-girdling faith. For the next thousand years there was a broad consensus that political and religious rulers ought to work together to foster Christian unity and to strike down dissent. Modern-day notions of a stark division between religious and secular concerns would not have played well in late antique and medieval Christendom—simple categories of Church and State, as presently understood, were not really operative. It was not unusual for lofty bishops to secure high political office, and more importantly, there was a firm belief that religious conformity was crucial to political and social order.

That said, there was still a distinction to be made between those who wielded what contemporaries often referred to as the two swords of religious and political power. The two camps developed a rare talent for squaring off against one another, but this is not the book in which to recount such tussles in any detail. Suffice to say that medieval Europe would see Holy Roman Emperors and French and English kings arguing with popes about the right to tax and appoint clerics and see those clerics quarrelling with local rulers about any number of judicial, territorial, and fiscal issues.

The relationship was uneasy, but hardly anyone doubted that it ought to exist. For all the awkward moments there was a shared assumption that religious and political leaders ought to be jointly responsible for enforcing a specific Christian agenda. The constant arguments were usually about the nuts and bolts of political and ecclesiastical influence: Should a local ruler be entitled to nominate his bishops, or was this always within the purview of the pope in Rome? Was it up to the pope alone to define doctrine, or was this not better left to a general council of the Church? Where did ultimate authority reside?

The fundamental idea—that Christian rulers and Christian clerics were part and parcel of a shared enterprise—was only rarely challenged, and when such challenges arose, they were routinely and vigorously attacked. It is also important to note that the dream of complete Christian uniformity remained in rude health. There was, so the theory went, only one authentic version of Christianity—usually derived from the pronouncements of the Church's earliest councils—and alternative ideas (often denounced as heresies) were deemed to be intolerable. This notion of the one true Church may very well have been a pipe dream, but a specific version of Christianity was to enjoy privileges and garner financial support from the entire population, and that population was obliged to attend its services. Religious pluralism was anathema: on this point, at least, Church and State were in complete agreement.

## REFORMATION

The medieval era witnessed any number of heretical challenges: provocative ideas about theology and ecclesiology had helped to define the age. Just occasionally—with the Cathars of 13th-century France and the Hussites of 15th-century Bohemia being only the most conspicuous examples—a vibrant religious alternative went a long way toward undermining the regional status quo. In spite of this, it is safe to say that, by the dawn of the 16th century, long-established notions about the interplay between religious and political power were still very much in the ascendant. With the Reformation protests of such men as Martin Luther and John Calvin, new vistas emerged, although there is space to question whether they were quite as radical as is often supposed.

The revolutionary nature of some aspects of the mainstream Reformation can easily be overstated. On the theological level, there were indeed some extraordinary innovations. There was talk of a priesthood of all believers and of relying solely on the words of Scripture rather than the man-made accretions of tradition. Into the bargain, novel ways of explaining how people might hope to achieve salvation were hammered out. Calvinists, for instance, introduced the notion of double predestination: some people were destined, by God's arbitrary decision, to reign in heaven, whereas others were destined for hell. The old, presumably comforting notion that one's behavior in the vale of tears could influence one's eternal prospects—that doing good works set one on the right track—was abandoned.

For all these departures, there was still considerable reluctance to allow a radical democratization of faith. The notion that someone had to be in charge of defining true religion and enforcing its parameters died hard. Even within Protestantism, there was little doubt that a complete divorcing of political and religious authority might very well result in chaos. On first inspection, the ideas of someone such as Luther seemed to open up the possibility of a theological free-for-all. If the monopoly of a clerical elite was to be dispensed with, and if every Christian was entitled to read Scripture (ideally in his or her own language), then all sorts of new avenues of Christian inquiry became possible.

The first leaders of the Reformation, not least Luther himself, soon began to dread the potential consequences. Accordingly, what historians often refer to as the magisterial (magistrate-led) Reformation came to the fore. The 16th century witnessed the emergence of many new Christian denominations, and Europe became divided, as never before, between competing Christian constituencies, but in the vast majority of cases, there was still an indomitable conviction that religious and political power ought to remain connected. The ideas might be new, but in the realm of their enforcement and protection, an older paradigm remained dominant.

Thus it was that in places such as England, Scandinavia, the corners of eastern Europe, and a host of German cities and principalities, a new breed of state churches emerged. Even in those places where old ecclesiastical arrangements were dispensed with, where bishops' dioceses gave way to local, independent congregations, where something we would now refer to as Presbyterianism gained ground, there was still a strong feeling that Christianity ought to guide every aspect of a polity's life. Religion and politics were still bedfellows.

In spite of all this, the more explosive political, social, and intellectual consequences of the Reformation could never quite be contained. Historians sometimes refer to a profoundly dangerous idea at the heart of the Protestant experiment. Some denizens of the 16th century felt emboldened to take the invitation to interrogate Scripture afresh at face value. As a result they conjured up innovative theological ideas and church structures of their own. Indubitably, this scandalized the Protestant mainstream, and many such groups— with the ill-fated Anabaptists leading the way—were solidly denounced. The trouble was, Protestantism always lacked a central locus of authority: it lacked something equivalent to Rome and the great church councils of Catholicism. The potential for fracture and fragmentation was colossal, and despite the efforts of the leaders of state-sponsored Protestantism, any number of vibrant, self-defining denominations sprang up during the 16th and 17th centuries.

This, self-evidently, represented a major challenge to the old certainties of Church–State cooperation. One version of Protestantism might secure state support, but in many places, there were other Protestant groups seeking to win over converts. Europe would find it hard to confront this new religious landscape, but it was in America that such groups as the Quakers, the Baptists, the Methodists, and many more besides provoked the greatest challenge to established ideas of religious orthodoxy and conformity.

It cannot be stressed enough that the idea of a single, politically sanctioned variety of Christianity ruling the theological roost traveled effortlessly across the Atlantic. This was perhaps inevitable. The vast majority of 17th-century American colonists were dedicated to enforcing uniformity in their particular corners of the newly settled continent. The notion that religious conformity was crucial to political and social order and that, at a fundamental level, it was the business of political leaders to sustain that conformity remained extremely fashionable. This was as true of the Congregationalists of Massachusetts as it was of the Anglicans of Virginia or the Dutch Reformed of New Netherland.

Unfortunately (at least for the syndics of local orthodoxies), sustaining this vision was much more difficult in the vast, chaotic territories of the New World than it had been back in Europe. The results were fascinating, and as reductive as such an analysis inevitably is, the history of Church–State relations in 17th- and 18th-century America can best be understood as a collision between those who believed that political and religious authority (though enjoying their distinctive spheres of influence) ought to share the burden of imposing a closely regulated Christianity and those (in a tiny, much-buffeted minority, at first) who sought out alternative ideas.

Members of the latter camp should not necessarily be seen as bold trailblazers of modern notions of religious freedom—they had a worldview that differed, in many particulars, from our own—but they undoubtedly set motions in trend that, with the addition of some abstract theorizing and the exigencies of living in an endlessly mutable colonial milieu, would transform revered ideas about Church and State.

The seeds of this curious conflict were there for all to see in the England out of which the American colonial adventure emerged.

## CROSSING THE ATLANTIC

America's debate about Church and State began in Tudor and Stuart England. Under Elizabeth I (reigned 1558–1603), James I (reigned 1603–1625), and Charles I (reigned 1625–1649), religion and politics were intimately connected. There was a single, national Church with the monarch at its head, and attendance at parish services was a requirement of law. Failure to take your seat in the pews every Sunday was met, at the very least, by financial penalties. One of the chief duties of the magistrate, both locally and nationally, was to enforce religious orthodoxy, and the old, venerable model of Church–State relations, regnant since the time of Constantine, was still very much in vogue.

Unfortunately, there was considerable disagreement about the sort of Church that England ought to have. During the reign of Henry VIII (reigned 1509–1547), England had cast off obedience to the pope, but in many ways, its theological identity had remained solidly Catholic. There had been some moves in the direction of reform, and the country's religious landscape had been transformed—the dissolution of the realm's monasteries provided striking evidence of this—but more radical, identifiably Protestant ideas had still struggled for air. This all changed under Henry's son, Edward VI (reigned 1547–1553). England became something of a refuge for harried continental reformers and witnessed liturgical innovation on an increasingly adventurous scale. With the arrival of Edward's half-sister Mary (reigned 1553–1558), the pendulum swung back, and the nation witnessed six years of Catholic revivalism. England returned to papal obedience, and vocal Protestants were pursued and persecuted with determination: almost 300 of them perished at the stake.

Given all these oscillations, it is hardly surprising that the next reign, that of Elizabeth I, was a time of profound religious confusion. An assaulted, but still extensive Catholic community sat alongside Protestant constituencies of varying agendas and aspirations. The Elizabethan religious settlement was very much a compromise. At a purely theological level, as articulated in the nation's articles of faith, it can be sensibly seen as quite advanced but, at the same time, many older ideas and ecclesiastical structures remained entrenched. There were still bishops, priests still wore distinctive vestments, and old practices—making the sign of the cross at various liturgical moments, kneeling at the communion rail, and so forth—could still be witnessed in parish churches across the country.

Some members of the English Church found these survivals distasteful. They referred to them as "dregs of popery," as indications that the English Church had not gone nearly far enough down the road of reform. To such people, the Church was, as the catchphrase had it, but half-reformed. These so-called Puritans (though such a catch-all term is not always especially useful) demanded more change. During Elizabeth's reign it was just about possible to contain the dissent, but during the first few decades of the 17th century, theological tempers soared, and an always simmering situation boiled over.

Various groups grew increasingly tired of "tarrying with the magistrate" and hoping for better days that showed no sign of arriving.

They decided to seek out new pastures. Many of them, starting with the Pilgrims who dropped anchor off the New England coast in the early 1620s, headed for America. These first arrivals in English America were at the radical end of the religious spectrum. They sought to divorce themselves from the homeland and to erect an entirely separate, determinedly exclusivist religious culture. Seeing them as harbingers of religious freedom and toleration is entirely erroneous. Those of slightly more conservative tastes followed them to the Bay Colony, but both groups had one thing in common. A supreme irony lay ahead. People would travel thousands of miles across an ocean in order to escape marginalization and even persecution. But once they arrived, they set about establishing religious cultures that were every bit as committed to enforcing uniformity and striking down dissent as those from which they had fled.

To add even more puzzlement to the mix, America was not merely a refuge for disenchanted Puritans. It would also become home to devoted supporters of the Anglican status quo, to Catholics, to members of the Calvinist Dutch Reformed Church, and in time, a dazzling array of other Christian denominations and followers of non-Christian faiths. Given these circumstances, vigorous debates about Church and State were always destined to be part of the American colonies' birthright.

## SUGGESTED READING

Of the many surveys of the Reformation period, Diarmaid MacCulloch, *Reformation: Europe's House Divided* (London, 2003), and Euan Cameron, *The European Reformation* (New York, 1991), are especially recommended. Those requiring a briefer summary should turn to Peter Marshall, *Reformation: A Very Short Introduction* (Oxford, 2009).

On Reformation theology, Alister McGrath's *Reformation Thought: An Introduction* (3rd ed., Cambridge, MA, 1999) is still a reliable first port of call. On the English Reformation in particular, see Christopher Haigh, *English Reformations. Religion, Politics and Society under the Tudors* (Oxford, 1993); Felicity Heal, *Reformation in Britain and Ireland* (New York, 2003); Nicholas Tyacke, *Aspects of English Protestantism. c. 1530–1700* (Manchester, 2001).

# 2

# 17th-Century Tumult

The 17th-century American colonies inherited many legacies from the European Reformation. Existing battles and confessional differences, including arguments about the ideal relationship between Church and State, were transported across the Atlantic Ocean. The always staggering fact is that so many different theological and ecclesiastical visions sat side by side.

The emerging Anglican denomination—made up of those who were broadly satisfied with the religious settlement crafted by the Elizabethan and Jacobean churches—found a home in many of the Southern colonies, preeminently in Virginia. In such places, the Anglican *via media*, its middle walking, proved very popular. Traditional parish structures and ecclesiastical arrangements gelled with a relatively conservative interpretation of the Reformation's theological consequences.

New England, meanwhile, was very much a Puritan heartland: home to both radical separatists and those who, though determined to erect a beacon of authentic Christianity (to build a city on a hill, as they famously put it), did not divorce themselves entirely from the religious ferment back home. In Massachusetts there was a keen sense of making things new, but also a hope that the example being set might be able to move things toward further, more complete Reformation in England.

At least for a while, the Dutch Reformed Church had a billet in New Netherland, and although the English-speaking colonies were a predominantly Protestant enterprise, in one locale (the decidedly curious colony of Maryland) a measure of religious toleration was, at least temporarily, extended to Roman Catholics.

During the 17th century, older ideas about the intersection between faith and politics often held sway. There would be radical departures—the Rhode Island of Roger Williams and the Pennsylvania of William Penn, which we will get to in short measure—but elsewhere, although theologies and church structures differed, there was a firm and only rarely challenged belief that, at some level, the entanglement of religious and secular affairs was still a good, and entirely necessary, idea. Similarly, churchmen were as accustomed as they ever had been to guiding public morality and to commenting on and influencing matters that we would now think of as distinctively secular.

In some colonies (Massachusetts being a good example), there was a consistent effort to define the specific spheres of influence inhabited by political leaders and clerics, but even here the notion that both groups were engaged in the shared work of building and sustaining a Christian commonwealth was normative. Later notions of Church–State separation were not to be countenanced.

The religious history of the 17th- and 18th-century American colonies is, at one level, the story of how this revered and robust conception of political-clerical cooperation competed with novel and extremely disruptive ideas about a more stark distinction between Church and State.

## VIRGINIA AND MASSACHUSETTS

The most obvious place to begin our survey is the colony of Virginia because, in many ways, its early decades amounted to an exercise in the root and branch transplantation of an existing vision of Church and State.

Although it soon became a state-run colony, answerable directly to the crown, Virginia began life as a private enterprise—the undertaking of the Virginia Company of London, chartered in November 1606. Even in these earliest years, however, there was a no doubt that sponsoring and expanding Christianity was at the heart of its mission. This was made abundantly clear in the colony's initial charter:

We, greatly commending, and graciously accepting of, their desires for the furtherance of so noble a work, which may, by the providence of Almighty God, hereafter tend to the glory of his Divine Majesty, in propagating of Christian religion to such people, as yet live in darkness and miserable ignorance of the true knowledge and worship of God . . . do, by these our letters patents, graciously accept of, and agree to, their humble and well-intended desires.

Similarly, among the king's instructions to the colony was the following commandment:

We do especially ordain, charge and require the said president and councils and the ministers of the said several colonies respectively, within their several limits, and precincts, that they, with all diligence, care, and respect, do provide, that the true word, and service of God and Christian faith be preached, planted, and used, not only within every of the said several colonies, and plantations, but also as much as they may amongst the savage people which do or shall adjoin unto them, or border upon them, according to the doctrine, rights, and religion now professed and established within our realm of England; and that they shall not suffer any person, or persons to withdraw any of the subjects or people inhabiting, or which shall inhabit within any of the said several colonies and plantations from the same.

With the arrival of direct crown supervision from London in 1624, matters became increasingly codified. Ministers, who oversaw traditional parish structures, were supported by public funds, and any cleric who wanted to preach in the colony required a license from the local authorities. Just as in England, every inhabitant was expected to attend church services, and those who failed to comply faced various punishments. It was declared in 1624 that "whosoever shall absent himself from divine service any Sunday without an allowable excuse shall forfeit a pound of tobacco, and he that absent himself a month shall forfeit fifty pounds of tobacco." This might strike us a rather curious penalty, but in 17th-century Virginia tobacco-growing was one of the lynchpins of the local economy. To lose 50 pounds of this precious commodity was a huge blow.

Virginia adopted the doctrinal and liturgical standards of the English Church—its Prayer Book and its Thirty-Nine Articles—and there were many indications of the close relationship between religious and political authority. When newly appointed clerics arrived in the colony, they were expected to present themselves to the governor, who then duly inducted them into office.

Imposing this familiar structure on Virginia was not straightforward. Back in England there had always been complaints about the "dark corners" of the realm: those places, geographically distant from the seats of political authority, in which religious dissent was apt to thrive. It was even harder to enforce conformity in Virginia. In comparison with their English equivalents, Virginian parishes were huge, and a single minister often would have to cover a great deal of ground in order to fulfill his parochial duties. It is also true that the standard of the Virginian clergy was not always, shall we say, stellar. This point has sometimes been exaggerated in the scholarly literature, but it remains a fairly obvious point that the competent, well-trained Anglican minister would be much more likely to seek out a living in a comfortable English parish than in a wilderness thousands of miles across the ocean. There was also the small matter of Virginia lacking any *in situ* bishops: a state of affairs that would concern Anglican colonists well into the 18th century.

All of these factors created a religious environment that, on paper, was well defined and obsessed with conformity and in which the local authorities were devoted to pouncing on religious dissent or the arrival of an unsanctioned minister or preacher. In practice, however, Virginia was sufficiently large and unregulated for dissenting groups to establish themselves.

As we will see, by the middle of the 18th century, the persistence of groups such as the Baptists continued to infuriate the Virginian authorities. It was no coincidence that some of the most energetic advocates of legislative change, men such as Madison and Jefferson, were Virginians. They knew from firsthand experience that imposing and sustaining a very English vision of Church–State relations had never quite worked in Virginia: dissenters kept cropping up, only to face prosecution. For people such as Madison and Jefferson, this was an intolerable state of affairs: a recipe, by their calculation, for social fracture and disaffection.

This was the future, however. As cumbersome as it sometimes was, the Virginian approach to Church–State affairs, shared by the other Anglican colonies of the South, won broad support among the colony's population. Virginia was the least innovative but one of the most robust early American colonies. For the vast majority of Virginians, it simply made good sense to mirror the ecclesiastical and theological identity of the place from which they had traveled.

More than that, even when the homeland edged toward a more inclusive attitude—as with the expansion of religious tolerance in the wake of the English 1688–1689 revolution—Virginia often resisted such trends. Right up to the eve of American independence, being anything other than an Anglican in Virginia was a perilous pursuit. We will learn more about this when we meet figures such as John Leland, Samuel Davies, and of course, Jefferson and Madison as this chapter continues. Paradoxically, the colony that was perhaps most concerned with sustaining the status quo turned out to be the most influential crucible of change.

***

In the colonies to the north, heated arguments about toleration and Church–State relations were evident from the outset. Massachusetts is a case in point. In the Bay Colony, there was scant appetite for many aspects of the Anglican tradition. As already mentioned, the very first pilgrims to New England (who, it ought to be recognized, embodied the very antithesis of tolerationist thinking) were determined to separate themselves entirely from the English Church. Those who followed during the 1630s and 1640s did not abandon all links with the home country. There was a constant dialogue between center and periphery, and during the era of the English Civil War, many New England luminaries (not least Roger Williams) involved themselves with ecclesiastical debates in the homeland. Nonetheless, one of the defining characteristics of the residents of Massachusetts was that they were eager to erect a new, improved, and by their standards, truly Christian commonwealth.

In 1629 it fell to John Winthrop, soon to be the governor of Massachusetts, to articulate this vision. His famous reasons for removal made it abundantly clear that the churches of the New World were embarking on a bold religious experiment. The sense of leaving behind the corrupt past was plain for all to see. According to Winthrop, the churches of Europe "are brought to desolation, and our sins, for which the Lord begins already to frown upon us, and to cut us short, do threaten evil times to be coming upon us." It was sensible to seek out a "refuge for many whom he means to save out of the general calamity." God clearly had "some great work in hand which he hath revealed to his prophets among us whom he hath stirred up to encourage his servants to this plantation."

People such as Winthrop had grown disenchanted with the progress, or lack thereof, within the English Church. From the late 1620s, those of more radical sympathies began to voice their distaste for a new species of "popishly affected" bishops, who openly criticized Calvin's doctrines of predestination and who sought to focus their congregations' attentions on the altar and the sacramental majesty of Holy Communion—diverting their attention, so it was alleged, from the true focal point of any reputable Protestant religious ceremony: the pulpit and the sermon.

As the 1630s progressed, scrupulous Sabbath observance in England gave way to the official sanctioning of games and dancing on Sundays, and moveable communion tables were replaced in many churches by fixed, railed-off altars. For those who had long been complaining about the inadequacies of the Book of Common Prayer and who resented ritualistic practices that reminded them of the Catholic past, such developments were the final straw. The ascension of William Laud to the see of Canterbury in 1633 was seen as the culmination of unhealthy trends that had been gathering momentum ever since Charles I had become king in 1625.

It is important to stress that, whatever his critics might have suggested, William Laud was no kind of papist-in-disguise. He did not smash a Calvinist consensus because, outside of certain university and intellectual circles, no such consensus existed. However, what the changes in England's religious identity certainly did achieve was the further alienation of the kinds of

Protestants who began to look toward America as a religious haven. Many of them ended up in Boston.

Massachusetts was built on the idea of Congregationalism. Instead of traditional ecclesiastical structures, governed by bishops, there was to be a network of individual, largely self-governing local congregations that jealously guarded their autonomy. Within this scheme it was also important to make a distinction between the roles and responsibilities of religious and political dignitaries. As William Bradshaw had explained in 1605, "no ecclesiastical minister ought to exercise or accept any civil public jurisdiction and authority, but ought to be wholly employed in spiritual office and duties to that congregation over which he is set."

This was all decidedly radical, and it had a significant impact on Church–State relations. Historians sometimes used to describe 17th-century Massachusetts as a theocracy—a place in which clerics dominated the political landscape. This was a wrongheaded analysis. As Bradshaw's statement makes clear, New England Puritans were often determined to avoid the less seemly aspects of secular and religious entanglement. The pollution of spiritual matters by worldly concerns was one of the mistakes they were determined to avoid. For them, it was the hallmark of popery.

They also saw sense in granting local congregations a great deal of initiative. So far as disciplinary matters were concerned, the punishment of minor offenses was usually left to local communities. Nor did committing a religious offense (the sort of misdeed that might require excommunication) necessarily lead to a person's alienation and exclusion from the political world. It was declared in 1641, for instance, that "no church censure shall degrade or depose any man from any civil dignity, office or authority he shall have in the commonwealth." To this extent, at least, religious and political matters were sometimes treated separately.

For all this, there was never any doubt in Massachusetts that faith and politics ought to enjoy a mutually enriching and very close relationship. At least at first, in order to be a fully fledged citizen of the colony—in order to be able to vote or hold political office—it was absolutely necessary to be a member of the Congregational Church. Nor was such Church membership a simple matter of attending religious services: individuals were expected to provide full and frank evidence that they had undergone a conversion process and that they showed all the likely signs of being among God's elect.

Furthermore, any church in the Bay Colony required governmental approval, and it was to be supported by taxes raised from among the general populace. That populace also had to be educated, and here the interaction between Church and State was perhaps most conspicuous. By the 1640s, elementary schools, supported by public funds, had begun to spring up across the colony, and their primary objective was to impart knowledge of Scripture.

The laws that governed religious life in Massachusetts were enacted by the colony's General Court, the legislative arm of the colony's government. It was therefore a governmental body that declared, in 1631, "that for time to come no man shall be admitted to the freedom of this body politic, but such as are members of some of the churches within the limits of the same." The same body, in 1635, declared that "whereas complaint hath been made to this Court that diverse persons within this jurisdiction do usually absent themselves from church meetings upon the Lord's day, power is therefore given to any two assistants to hear and ensure, either by fine or imprisonment . . . all misdemeanours of that kind committed by any inhabitant within this jurisdiction, provided they exceed not the fine of five shillings for one offence."

As for the boundary between secular and clerical authority, this was sometimes decidedly blurry. Eminent ministers became accustomed to intervening in political matters (as when a delegation of clerics helped to convince John Winthrop not to stand for yet another term as governor), and political leaders played a crucial role in attacking religious dissent. Although the workaday supervision of religious conformity was left to individual congregations, the arrival of a particularly threatening theological challenge required the direct intervention of the colony's political elite. At such moments, political and social order was deemed to be in jeopardy, and the magistrate was expected to play his part in calming the waters.

Such moments seemed to crop up very frequently in 17th-century Massachusetts, and they usually coincided with the arrival of members of dissenting Protestant denominations. In 1651, the Baptists John Clarke, Obadiah Holmes, and John Crandall arrived in the town of Lynn after a three-day walk from Rhode Island. After engaging in preaching and baptizing, they were arrested and offered the option of paying fines or facing more gruesome punishment. Two of the men raised the necessary funds, but Holmes refused to pay. He was tied to a post and whipped in Boston's marketplace.

A few years later, the Quaker Mary Dyer was arrested and banished from the colony. She returned, and in October 1659, she was sentenced to death by the General Court, along with her fellow Quakers William Robinson and Marmaduke Stevenson. The two men went to the gallows, but Dyer was granted a last-minute reprieve and banished from the colony. Undeterred, Dyer returned to Boston in 1660, but on this occasion, there was to be no escape. In May 1660 she was hanged on Boston Common.

These were very graphic of examples of the state intervening in order to preserve its vision of religious conformity and to stamp out dissent (and we might well perceive the infamous Massachusetts witch-craze, later in the century, as another salient example of this tendency). For our present purposes, two more causes célèbres, the trials and banishments of Anne Hutchinson and Roger Williams, help to bring this issue (the wellspring of many debates about Church and State) into even sharper relief.

## HUTCHINSON AND WILLIAMS

Anne Hutchinson was precisely the sort of person who, during the first decades of the 17th century, had grown weary of England's version of the Protestant Reformation. Her father, Francis, had been a disgruntled minister who, though conforming during most of his career, had once suffered censure and imprisonment after criticizing the poor training offered to England's clergy and the political machinations that so frequently influenced ministerial appointments. Anne herself was certainly located at the more radical end of the Protestant spectrum, and she and her husband William would travel considerable distances in order to hear suitably puritanical preaching. They were prime candidates for a trip across the Atlantic Ocean, and in May 1634, they boarded the *Griffin*, bound for Massachusetts.

Anne was never bashful about voicing her dissent, and during the ocean crossing, she found time to criticise the preaching of the minister Zechariah Symmes. More disruption was to follow. The Hutchinsons began to organize weekly meetings in their home, during which groups of colonists gathered to discuss recent sermons. These proved to be very popular, and by 1637, as many as 70 people were participating.

On the face of things, this might look like just the sort of introspective religious activity that a godly commonwealth would applaud. Unfortunately, the local authorities, who had become sufficiently concerned to send their own eavesdroppers to the meetings, were very suspicious of the things being discussed by Anne and her acolytes. Here, the close interaction between Church and political concerns came into the sharpest focus. When troublesome theological postures arose, they were perceived as a threat, not just to people's consciences and devotional well-being, but to the stability of the social and political order. Anne Hutchinson was seen as just such a threat, and in the process of censure, trial, and banishment that she endured, the political authorities of Massachusetts played a conspicuous role.

Hutchinson was audacious enough to dip her toe into some especially controversial theological pools: debates about grace, free will, and humankind's quest for salvation. Few questions were more contentious within the Protestant fraternity. For those of Calvinist sympathies, humankind had nothing much do with the running of the salvific economy. God, in entirely arbitrary fashion, had long ago decided who was to be saved and who was to be damned. People could strive to make themselves look and feel godly, but their feeble human efforts lacked any agency. This was apt to provoke bleak and puzzled responses. What was a person to do if he had convinced himself that he was among the reprobate and unable to change his hell-bound trajectory?

No genuine Calvinist ever suggested that human effort could coerce God or that a person could *cause* his or her salvation. Salvation was always about the arrival of wholly unmerited grace in the souls of undeserving people. That said, some theologians wondered if it was at least possible for human beings to *cooperate* with grace, perhaps even to *prepare* their hearts for its arrival.

Many influential members of the Congregational Church answered this question in the affirmative. Good works, they argued, did not *cause* salvation, but if a person behaved in godly fashion, then perhaps this might be taken as a *sign* that grace had descended on him or her. Anne Hutchinson and her followers found such ideas risible. The notion of cooperation with grace was soundly denounced: grace, they said, arrived unbidden, and human action, even if perceived as enjoying a supporting, cooperative role, was of no account. Nor was there any covenant of works, only a covenant of grace. Supposing that a person's behavior might indicate his or her prospects in the afterlife was arrogant and theologically misguided.

This might strike us as rather obscure religious speculation, and we might wonder why it was seen as such a palpable threat to political and social order. It is important to remember, however, that these were troubled times for Massachusetts. The government in England was making threatening noises about repealing the colony's charter. As a result, local leaders were unusually sensitive to any internal rabble-rousing. That Hutchinson managed to win over some lofty members of the political establishment made her even more threatening. It was also a period of strained relations with the indigenous population. The fact that some of Hutchinson's supporters refused to join in the colony's military engagements with the Pequot Indians did not help their cause. More than anything else, however, Hutchinson alarmed the local authorities because of the practical, political consequences of what she was saying and because of the personal nature of some of her attacks. Worse yet, so far as her contemporaries were concerned, she was a woman.

In consequence, the wolves, both clerical and secular, were unleashed. Hutchinson's insistence that those who were truly living under a covenant of grace enjoyed direct contact with God was wholly unacceptable to orthodox opinion. Such intimate revelation was thought to have ended in the apostolic era, and Hutchinson's suggestion that an individual could have direct knowledge of God's will struck some as a challenge to the accepted Protestant belief that the Bible was the fundamental source of religious knowledge. Her most unwelcome claim was that those who had truly received the gift of grace could tell who was playing a wily game of hypocritical subterfuge. By Hutchinson's calculation there were many such people in Massachusetts, and she did not shy away from revealing that almost every teacher and minister in the colony was a bad theologian and, quite possibly, lacking in sanctifying grace. Almost every member of the local clergy and local political elite was portrayed as a worthless hypocrite.

This all had disturbing repercussions for the social status quo. Massachusetts prided itself on being a godly commonwealth peopled by God-fearing souls united by bonds of Christian love, but here was Hutchinson calling into question the characters of the leaders of that commonwealth. She was questioning the validity of the entire political and clerical order.

After attempts at damage control (meeting with Hutchinson in October and December 1636), Massachusetts turned, as Americans often still turn in such matters, to the courts, and the man in charge of the proceedings was no less a political luminary than the colony's governor. Church and State mounted the steps of judicial adjudication hand-in-hand.

"Mrs Hutchinson," John Winthrop began, "you are called here as one of those that have troubled the peace of the commonwealth and the churches here; you are known to be a woman that has had a great share in the promoting and divulging of those opinions that are causes of this trouble."

You have spoken divers things, as we have been informed very prejudicial to the honour of the churches and ministers thereof, and you have maintained a meeting and an assembly in your house that has been condemned by the general assembly as a thing not tolerable nor comely in the sight of God nor fitting for your sex, and notwithstanding . . . you have continued the same. Therefore we have thought good to send for you to understand how things are, that if you be in an erroneous way we may reduce you that so you may become a profitable member here among us, otherwise if you be obstinate in your course that then the court may take such course that you may trouble us no further.

As for the unauthorized meetings in Hutchinson's house, the court was blunt: "By what warrant do you continue such a course?" Hutchinson reached for scriptural sanction: "I conceive there lies a clear rule in *Titus*, that the elder women should instruct the younger and then I must have a time wherein I must do it." In response to this, Winthrop suggested that Hutchinson was grossly misinterpreting the text: all it really implied was that the elder woman is there to teach the younger about their wifely business and about how to honor their husbands. Hutchinson was unconvinced: What, she asked, if younger women came to her to be instructed in the ways of God? Was she to turn them away?

Winthrop was having none of it:

We find such a course as this to be greatly prejudicial to the state . . . those meetings . . . and your opinions being known to be different from the word of God may seduce many simple souls that resort unto you, besides that the occasion which has come of late has come from none but such as have frequented your meetings, so that now they are flown off from magistrates and ministers . . . And besides that it will not well stand with the commonwealth that families should be neglected for so many neighbors and dames . . . We see no rule of God for this, we see not that any should have authority to set up any other exercises besides what authority has already set up.

Hutchinson's response was bold: "Sir, I do not believe that to be so." Present some rule in Scripture that supports such a position, she urged, and then she would accept what her accusers had to say. An angry Winthrop reminded Hutchinson that they were *her* judges, not the other way round.

Next into the fray was the deputy governor, Thomas Dudley. He reminded the court of Hutchinson's turbulent past: from criticizing preachers during her sea voyage to the colony to openly denouncing almost every minister in Boston. Hutchinson was repeatedly charged with criticizing the covenant of works and its adherents, and she was clearly most resented because she had traduced the magistrates and ministers of the community.

Up to this point Hutchinson had been doing rather well, fending off her accusers with wit and theological savvy. But then she made a fatal error of judgment. Hutchinson explained that she had always been able to distinguish between true and false ministry. Deputy Governor Dudley asked the obvious question: how? By an immediate revelation, Hutchinson replied. And thus a day and a half of skillful, cautious testimony suddenly counted for nothing. Such talk of immediate revelation was always destined to seem intolerable to a courtroom of 17th-century New England Puritans. "Mrs Hutchinson," Winthrop announced, "the sentence of the court . . . is that you are banished from out of our jurisdiction as being a woman not fit for our society." "I desire to know wherefore I am banished," pleaded Hutchinson. "Say no more," Winthrop replied, "the court knows wherefore and is satisfied."

It was an epochal moment, during which the role of political authority in policing religious orthodoxy and punishing extreme religious dissent was loudly bruited. Hutchinson was adjudged to have stirred up unnecessary theological strife and speculation. She had poured scorn on the clerical and political establishment, and along the way, she had won over some very notable residents of Massachusetts to her cause. In the preceding couple of years, this had provoked stark divisions that had played a major role in the colony's routine political elections. As reward for all this, Hutchinson was banished from the colony, and many of the guardians of both Church and State let out a sigh of relief.

It would be wrong to see Hutchinson simply as a maverick. It could be argued that in some regards (though these would not include her talk of direct revelation), she was militating for a more authentic, more rigorous interpretation of Calvinist theology. If anything, it was the supporters of a covenant of works and those who talked about cooperating with grace who were playing fast and loose with the Calvinist legacy. This did not matter a bit to the Massachusetts authorities, however. Hutchinson's ideas were deemed to be disruptive. Later chapters in this book document much talk of a compelling state interest in limiting freedom of expression. The denizens of 17th-century Massachusetts would not have put it that way (how could they, given that such phrasing is an invention of 20th-century jurisprudence?), but *mutatis mutandis,* the logic was not so very different.

Hutchinson was found guilty of overstepping the line between private speculation and public nuisance. From our perspective, her treatment might well seem unfair; from the perspective of the time, it was deemed necessary. If nothing else, her story reveals that however unique and however groundbreaking the Bay Colony strove to be, it was still loyal to an established paradigm of Church–State relations. Sometimes, those who wielded political power were duty-bound to pluck out the weeds of religious dissent.

\*\*\*

Hutchinson's post-banishment narrative ended in tragedy. After the death of her husband William in 1642, Anne and her children moved to Dutch territory in present-day Westchester County. A year later, Anne and 15 members of her family were massacred by local Indians. Much to his discredit, her nemesis John Winthrop crowed that this was a sure indication of divine retribution. Ultimately, beyond inspiring and infuriating her contemporaries, Hutchinson never managed to secure any lasting, concrete victories.

This could not be said of another resident of the Bay Colony who aggravated the local authorities every bit as much as Hutchinson and who endured the same kinds of strictures and banishment. His name was Roger Williams, and he would make an astonishingly durable contribution to American debates about Church and State, so much so that his name still routinely crops up in debates about the interplay of faith and politics. Such invocations are not always helpful, and they routinely ride roughshod over historical accuracy, but they pay testimony to the fact that Williams made a lasting mark.

\*\*\*

Williams arrived in America in 1631. Just like Anne Hutchinson, he had long harbored profound misgivings about the theological character of the English Church, and he wanted to separate himself from its activities as completely as possible. He therefore had little sympathy for those in Massachusetts (and they were certainly in the majority) who sustained hopes of reforming the homeland by means of transatlantic example.

Almost as soon as his ship dropped anchor in New England, Williams asserted his radical views and declined to take up any ecclesiastical position in Boston: he perceived it as a halfway, unseparated town. Instead, he headed to the separatist haven of Plymouth, 40 miles or so to the south, and spent two years serving as assistant to the pastor Ralph Smith. By 1633 he was to be found in Salem, assisting the minister Samuel Skelton and continuing his withering critique of everything that he found offensive in the New England religious experiment.

In a sense, Roger Williams was an unlikely champion of religious freedom. Throughout his long and turbulent colonial career, he was a decidedly uncompromising character, and he never shied away from denouncing the theological positions of those with whom he disagreed. There was a supreme irony in the fact that the man who did more than any other early 17th-century American figure to invigorate debate about religious freedom and Church–State relations was something of a theological snob. The great champion of toleration (as he is now so often depicted) had more than his fair share of intolerant moments.

There was much that Williams disliked about the Bay Company's activities. He argued against the granting of royal land patents to territories that had been seized from the indigenous population. He refused to accept the idea that unregenerate individuals should be allowed to take oaths of submission to the colony (something that all men above the age of 16 were expected to do). The name of God, he argued, should really not be heard on the lips of people still drowning in sin. Still more provocatively, and here the nub of Williams' contribution to Church–State debates began to take shape, he questioned the right of secular magistrates to punish various religious offenses—not least breaches of the first four Mosaic commandments.

So far as Williams was concerned, the state had no business intervening in the affairs of the Church. Any true religious body was built on the foundation of God's love. The authority of the State, by contrast, was always underpinned by the threat of force. So far as regulating a person's workaday life, this threat of force was perfectly legitimate (Williams himself would happily utilize it in his own colony of Rhode Island). In the sphere of religious belief, however, Williams saw the notion of coercion as both noxious and impractical. It was impossible to force someone to believe a particular idea: that was simply not how faith operated. As Williams, always capable of coining the telling phrase, put it, forced worship stank in the nostrils of God. He did not assert this because of a modern belief in religious pluralism: for Williams it was a matter of basic theological logic. It goes without saying that the political and clerical leaders of Massachusetts (who still held faith in the notion that religious belief could be coerced into shape) found Williams's stance deeply offensive.

In July 1635, Williams's opinions were denounced as "erroneous and very dangerous." Williams could not easily be removed from his clerical position in Salem, but Boston could still apply political pressure on the town, holding up decisions about requested land grants and even preventing deputies from Salem from taking up their seats in the General Court. Salem was outraged at such treatment and protested accordingly, with Williams urging the town to separate entirely from the colony, a suggestion that was far too radical for almost everyone. Finally, in October 1635, the court voted to banish him, accusing him of spreading sedition and heresy.

***

As already mentioned, there are serious risks involved in positioning Williams as a trailblazer of modern ideas about pluralism and religious freedom—although, goodness knows, this happens all the time. In fact, his ideas about separating Church and State (while passionately held) were rather different from our own. At their core was the notion that it was crucial to distinguish between the pure, spiritual realm and the impure, corrupt secular world. This, in turn, was based on a decidedly bleak, theologically motivated worldview that was very much of its time.

What cannot be gainsaid, however, is that in the wake of his banishment, Williams established a colony in which religious toleration was experimented with as never before in the American colonies. It is unsurprising that Americans look back on the founding of Rhode Island as one of the staging posts on the road to later, more expansive religious freedoms.

The 1638 social compact adopted by Williams's new community asserted a bold principle: individuals were obliged to abide by all public orders intended to sustain the public good—but only in *civil* matters. But what the people of Rhode Island thought and how they worshipped was their own business. There was to be "soul liberty" for every individual; there was to be no direct linkage between Church and State, no "enforced uniformity"; and "no man should be molested for his conscience."

Williams's arguments were further elucidated in a series of provocative tracts (including his *Queries of Highest Consideration, The Bloudy Tenent of Persecution,* and *The Bloudy Tenent Yet More Bloudy*). Williams insisted that his critics were making a host of basic theological and ecclesiastical mistakes: the sort of gaffes, Williams argued, that had been replicated throughout the long and bloody history of Christianity.

Civil authority, he explained, was an extraordinarily important component of human society, but it was (or should be) limited. Political rulers had the obvious duty of "making, publishing, and establishing of wholesome civil laws." Such laws promoted civil justice, punished wrongdoers, and provided a society with peace and security. This was also very good for the Christian faith; it promoted the "free passage of true religion." Outward civil peace, after all, was a great help to people who wanted to go about their worshipping as they saw fit. To this extent, at least (although it never involved direct entanglement with, or intervention in, specifically religious affairs), the State helped the Church (or churches) by creating a stable society.

Secular government was also charged with overseeing the election and appointment of the officers who were to devise and enforce such civil laws, and it had a duty to punish those who transgressed them. Similarly, when the civil peace was seriously threatened from either without or within, it was up to the secular authorities to ensure security and supervise the taking up of arms.

Williams was adamant, however, that the competence of civil authority stretched exactly this far and no further. As Williams wrote, "all civil states with their officers of justice in their respective constitutions and administrations are proved essentially civil, and therefore not judges, governors, or defenders of the spiritual or Christian state and worship." For one thing, and we have seen Williams making this point already, religious belief had nothing whatever to do with coercion: to be authentic it had to be free. It was therefore impossible for civil authority—which was always underpinned by the potential threat of force—to have any legitimate role in convincing individuals to subscribe to a particular belief or sect.

The efforts of secular authorities to impose uniformity of belief by means of threats and punishments were wrongheaded and invariably ended in disaster. The "weapons which are used by persecutors"—all the stocks, whips, prisons, swords, gibbets, and stakes—were of no use whatsoever against the spiritual strongholds that resided in the souls of men. Only "spiritual artillery and weapons" were appropriate, and these were exclusively in the hands and arsenal of God.

As soon as states became involved in defining and enforcing religious truth, the consequences were doleful. Jesus Christ, Williams insisted, had never asked that "the blood of so many hundred thousand souls of Protestants and Papists [be] spilled in the wars of present and former ages" for their respective consciences. Nor had he ever asked for "a uniformity of religion to be enacted and enforced in any civil state; which enforced uniformity (sooner or later) is the greatest occasion of civil war, ravishing of conscience, persecution of Christ Jesus in his servants, and of the hypocrisy and destruction of millions of souls."

Williams knew his Reformation history well, and his deeply held theological beliefs often segued into pragmatism. The state imposing a specific vision of Christianity was not only theologically disreputable; it also resulted in unnecessary strife and division.

Therefore, for reasons both theological and practical, it was simply better that "magistrates, as magistrates, have no power of setting up the form of church government, electing church officers, punishing with church censures." This logic had some extraordinary consequences. It was not even necessary for a secular ruler to be a Christian, a truly radical suggestion during the middle of the 17th century. Ultimately, the magistrate, "whether he receive Christianity before he be set in office, or whether he receive Christianity after . . . receives no more power of magistracy than a magistrate that has received no Christianity."

Williams also saw this separation of Church and State as a two-way street. Politicians should stay out of religion, but clerics should also keep out of politics. Williams conceded that although the Church could certainly help to "cast a blush of civility and morality" on the people, it was equally desirable that

the churches as churches, have no power . . . of erecting or altering forms of civil government, electing of civil officers, inflicting civil punishments . . . as by deposing magistrates from their civil authority, or withdrawing the hearts of the people against them, to their laws, no more than to discharge wives, or children, or servants, from due obedience to their husbands, parents, or masters.

This was the other half of Church–State separation, the one that Americans have tended to overlook, although it still raises its head today. There is an obvious echo of Williams's talk of ministers "withdrawing the hearts of the people" from particular political figures in current-day tussles over religious leaders and organizations endorsing or denouncing electoral candidates. But more of that anon.

***

Williams was damning both the whole Massachusetts enterprise and all the European efforts to combine Church and State that had come before it. Unsurprisingly, his polemic met with many frowns in the colony that had recently banished him. Massachusetts was furious, and largely through the efforts of John Cotton, it mounted a rebuttal. In fact, the prolonged Cotton–Williams debate of the 1640s and 1650s represented the first great American Church–State showdown.

John Cotton had much in common with both Anne Hutchinson and Roger Williams. He too had grown disenchanted with the pace of religious change in England. He too had fled the realm in the hope of creating a purer, more authentic Christian commonwealth across the ocean. The difference was that Cotton was perfectly happy with the ecclesiastical arrangements and the limited interaction between Church and State that Massachusetts had adopted. More than that, he helped to create them.

Cotton had his tricky moments during the 1630s, not least because he seems to have had some sympathy for some of Anne Hutchinson's theological positions, but he also emerged as the chief architect of the New England way of proceeding. It was largely thanks to him that a process had emerged by the mid-1630s in which would-be Church-members were expected to furnish verbal proof of the genuine conversion experience that transformed them into full citizens of Massachusetts society. Cotton was also positively delighted with the prospect of attenuated Church–State interaction. It made sense to him that the colony's laws were derived from biblical commandments, that ministers commented on political events, and that their counsel was routinely sought by municipal leaders.

As well as holding forth on everything from economic policy to the just price to land-grants, Cotton would be among those clergymen who attempted to articulate the colony's legal principles. His "Model of Moses His Judicials" was rejected in October 1636, but it would go on to form the basis of the laws of New Haven. He would presumably have agreed with Uriah Oakes, a Cambridge minister and early president of Harvard, who insisted that "the interest of righteousness in the commonwealth and holiness in the churches are inseparable . . . to divide what god hath conjoined . . . is folly."

Cotton did not want to replicate the mistakes of Europe, of course. He believed in some measure of State–Church separation: ministers were not eligible to serve in secular office, for instance, and as Cotton explained to John Davenport, it was important to distinguish "between the two administrations or polities, ecclesiastical and civil, which men commonly call the church and the commonwealth." The ecclesiastical administration was a "divine order appointed to believers" for the arrangement of "holy things." Civil administrators, by contrast, represented a "human order" intended to preserve "human souls in outward honour, justice and peace." It was crucial that these administrations not be confounded together by giving, for instance, any direct spiritual power to civil magistrates.

None of this meant that Cotton appreciated Williams's criticisms of Massachusetts. Cotton was determined to portray the colony as an idealized Christian commonwealth, a sacred covenant between man and God, in which blessings would be exchanged for the people's willingness to act justly, to love mercy, and to walk humbly with their creator. It was a special congregation, founded on Christian love and bonds of brotherly affection—just like those of the early Church—in which a certain kind of soul-searching spirituality, a distinct social ethic, and a social structure rooted in the town and the godly family would be normative. Cotton worked very hard to portray Massachusetts as a dream come true, and for him, Williams was the worst of gadflies.

In works such as *The Keys of the Kingdom of Heaven* (1644), *The Way of the Churches of Christ in New England* (1645), and *The Grounds and Ends of the Baptism of the Children of the Faithful* (1647), Cotton sought to convince an international audience of his colony's vitality and validity. Undermining Williams was a key aspect of this task. To Williams's *Mr Cotton's Letter Lately Printed* (1644), Cotton responded with *A Reply to Mr Williams* (1647). Then, in works such as *The Bloody Tenet, Washed and Made White in the Blood of the Lamb* (1647), Cotton set about challenging Williams's radical notion of complete "soul liberty" by insisting that there were occasions when a dissenter who publicly and repeatedly dissented from the generally held views of the community ought to be punished. There were moments (and Williams and Hutchinson had provoked two of them) when individual dissent was such a threat to social order that it had to be attacked.

This was not always easy for Cotton, and during the Hutchinson affair, he undoubtedly vacillated. Ultimately, however, he declined to leap to Hutchison's defense. In such extreme circumstances, it was not the exclusive preserve of the Church to deal with troublesome individuals; the state could, on occasion, play a part as well. Williams's desire that the two spheres of human society (the religious and the secular) be entirely separate was, Cotton believed, the consequence of poor theology. of the belief that, in preparation for the Second Coming of Christ, there should be an absolute division between matters of the body and matters of the spirit, between the filthiness of the world and the purity of the soul.

Cotton anticipated the Second Coming as well (such notions were decidedly modish during the 17th century), but he was adamant that, until it manifested itself, such fissures were entirely wrongheaded. For Cotton, a godly commonwealth, in which people fulfilled their duties to both Christ and mankind and to the institutions of civil and ecclesiastical authority, was wholly attainable in the here and now. In the effort to achieve such a goal, there was absolutely nothing wrong with religious and political leaders making common cause. Such cooperation was essential.

This was the nub of the controversy between Cotton and Williams. For Cotton, Massachusetts had gone far enough in making things new. For Williams, it had fallen short of godly expectation. Williams never queried the idea that Christian ideas ought to provide the bedrock of morality and public policy. Nor did he ever argue against a strong, interventionist civil government. Much to Williams's disappointment, Rhode Island was never easy to govern, and in civil matters, he recurrently argued in favor of an iron governmental fist. In a letter of 1655, Williams explained that the pursuit of the common good sometimes had to override the needs and desires of individuals. Think of the captain of a ship, Williams advised his readers. He had absolutely no authority over his passengers' beliefs, but to keep his ship on course, he had to be allowed to supervise their actions and punish their transgressions.

> The commander of this ship ought to command the ship's course, yea, and also command that justice, peace and sobriety, be kept and practiced, both among the seamen and all the passengers. If any of the seamen refuse to perform their services, or passengers to pay their freight; if any refuse to help, in person or purse, towards the common charges or defence; if any refuse to obey the common laws and orders of the ship, concerning their common peace or preservation; if any shall mutiny and rise up against their commanders and officers; if any should preach or write that there ought to be no commanders or officers, because all are equal in Christ . . . in such cases, whatever is pretended, the commander or commanders may judge, resist, compel and punish such transgressors, according to their deserts and merits.

No one in Massachusetts would have disagreed with this argument or blanched at the analogy. All agreed that ships, and states, ought to have brigs. The difference between Williams and his critics was that Williams limited the purview of political leaders. As soon as they intervened in matters of faith, as soon as they concerned themselves with the well-being of souls instead of bodies and goods, tragedy was likely to ensue. There would be conflict, and crucially, the forced conformity of the citizenry would not be worth a damn. What happens when people are forced to conform to ideas with which they disagree? Perhaps it would result in deceit: it would cause them "to play the hypocrite and dissemble in their religion, and to turn and return with the tide as all experience in the nations of the world doth testify." Alternatively, it would make them mad and more obdurate, producing "a brawny and steely hardiness from their suffering of their consciences." For Williams, neither option was desirable.

Roger Williams was not a Jeffersonian separatist ahead of his time. He once wrote about guarding against any "gap in the hedge or wall of separation between the garden of the Church and the wilderness of the world." Inevitably, this brings to mind a more famous metaphor of the wall of separation between Church and State invoked by the sage of Monticello. It would be foolish, however, to assume that Williams and Jefferson were singing from the same philosophical hymn-sheet. They simply were not. Jefferson was the child of Enlightenment and the disciple of Locke.

Williams had heard of none of these things. His vision of Church–State separation was rooted in biblical exegesis: essentially he wanted to protect religious faith and the life of the spirit from the intrusions of the poisonous, fleshly world. If a time machine could be pressed into service, and if Jefferson and Williams were allowed to meet, they would disagree, profoundly, about almost everything.

There is therefore room to lament the ways in which Williams's legacy has been recruited and abused through the centuries. His reasons for supporting the separation of Church and State were entirely different from those of the 20th and 21st centuries. That said, the abuse and the recruitment are easily understandable. Roger Williams believed that he was returning Christianity to its purest origins; rather than making things new, he was trying to make things ancient and authentic. But along the way, he created a colony that enjoyed unparalleled levels of religious toleration. Historical happenstance meant that, over the coming few decades, a belief in such toleration gained considerable ground in the American colonies. Williams's Rhode Island experiment, idiosyncratic as it might have been, was too good a precedent to ignore. Thus the grumpy, world-hating, Bible-deep Roger Williams was turned into a prophet of a cause in which he never would have believed. Such are the ironies of history.

## WHITHER CHURCH AND STATE? MARYLAND AND NEW NETHERLAND

All of the preceding evidence leads us to a predictable conclusion. There were many ways of confronting the issue of Church–State relations in 17th-century America. We have seen Virginia holding faith with the Anglican model, Massachusetts combining radicalism with tried-and-trusted methods of containing dissent, and Roger Williams embarking on his unusual and routinely misunderstood odyssey. There is more chaos to add to the mix.

Take Maryland, for instance. In the midst of post-Reformation squabbles, the most unlikely of colonial enterprises unfolded. Thanks to the first and second Lords Baltimore, George and Cecil Calvert, a colony arose in which seemingly spectacular religious toleration was available. It even extended to Roman Catholics, a unique dispensation in Anglophone America. As the colony's founding documents put it,

Whereas the enforcing of the conscience in matters of religion has frequently fallen out to be of dangerous consequences in those commonwealths where it hath been practised . . . be it enacted that no person . . . within this province . . . professing to believe in Jesus Christ, shall be any ways troubled, molested or discountenanced for or in respect of his or her religion, nor in the free exercise thereof.

This was an extraordinarily broad commandment: *anyone* who believed in Christ. Moreover, the person who decided "wilfully to wrong, disturb, trouble, or molest" such a believer, be he Catholic or Protestant, would meet with monetary fines, and if he persisted, such an offender "shall be severely punished by public whipping and imprisonment."

From the perspective of evolving Church–State relations, this has limited importance. It was still within the gift of the state to punish those who broke the rules that protected individual religious belief: it was about a state-sponsored intolerance of intolerance. It also did not last for very long. By the early 1690s Maryland had become a royal colony, ruled directly from London,, and in short measure, an Anglican religious establishment took over the theological and ecclesiastical reins. Still, for its time, the initial Maryland project was rather extraordinary.

***

A little to the north, the colony of New Netherland (present-day New York) also had its part to play in 17th-century debates about Church–State relationships. It might be supposed that a Dutch colony in America would have been the resolute champion of broad religious freedom and an enemy of unnecessary Church–State entanglement. After all, advocates of religious freedom—the aforementioned Roger Williams and the soon-to-be-analyzed William Penn and James Madison among them—would hail the 17th-century Dutch Republic as a beacon of the benefits that ensued from respecting liberty of conscience. In the midst of his battles with John Cotton, for instance, Williams suggested that his opponent look at the wonders achieved there: a commitment to toleration had managed to transform Amsterdam from a "poor fishing village" into one of the cultural, economic, and intellectual capitals of the world.

In fact, this was a rose-tinted way of looking at things. The Dutch Republic emerged out of a prolonged struggle with Catholic Spain, and to be fair, it did provide unprecedented levels of toleration. As a result, it benefited from an unusually dynamic artistic, intellectual, and economic life. Those who sought to replicate the social benefits of religious tolerance were quick to suggest that this was no random coincidence. There was always a paradox at the heart of the Dutch religious settlement, however. A strict Calvinistic faith, institutionalized in the Dutch Reformed Church, was the cornerstone of the nation's religious life. And yet, thanks to provisions of the 1579 Union of Utrecht, there was a commitment to sustaining freedom of conscience.

This was bold, but the liberality of the Dutch Republic can easily be over-stated. Membership of the Reformed Church was only ever voluntary, and by the 1630s, Amsterdam even allowed Jews and Lutherans to erect public places of worship, but it was also true that those of dissenting faiths were largely excluded from political life. Moreover, and this is a crucial point, the Dutch were advocates only of *toleration,* and that was never the same thing as believing in unbridled religious freedom—a distinction explored further in this book's discussion of James Madison. Catholics, for instance, were undoubtedly granted more respite from persecution in Holland than in any other Protestant country, but that did not mean that they avoided harassment. Dutch faith in toleration was always more about pragmatism than principle. It simply made sense to admit to religious diversity and reap the social and economic benefits: toleration subdued potential inter-religious conflicts and was good for the public purse.

For all this, Holland was perceived as a beacon and a refuge. It was also assumed that the nation's outlook would be transferred to the burgeoning overseas empire. In one corner of the Dutch world, however, an energetic colonial administrator was working very hard at proving that assumption wrong.

In May 1645, Pieter Stuyvesant took up the position of Director-General of New Netherland. Throughout his period in office, Stuyvesant garnered a great deal of criticism because of his over-authoritarian style of leadership, although, in many workaday ways, he did not do a terrible job. In New Amsterdam (again, today's New York) he employed surveyors to lay out streets and establish workable property lines, secured the town against the risks of fire damage, reduced the number of domestic animals roaming the town's streets, and even built Manhattan's first pier. There was also a campaign to maintain public order, and along with ordinances against many varieties of antisocial behavior, Stuyvesant introduced the "Rattle Watch" in 1658—a fledgling police force with the right to "pursue, attack and capture . . . pirates and vagabonds" and to arrest "robbers or others who would wish to inflict injury and damage." He even sought to oversee economic life more closely and, as well as cracking down on smuggling, established a weekly municipal market and an annual cattle fair and introduced measures intended to regulate the brewing and baking industries.

The introduction of such measures was entirely necessary, but in the religious arena, Stuyvesant was markedly less popular. Stuyvesant was a staunch Calvinist and unflinchingly intolerant of other faiths. Church and State were both in his pocket, so to speak, and he acted accordingly. First there was the policing of public morality. Stuyvesant was determined to assault vice and to instill virtue; under his rule, it was illegal to buy alcohol after nine o'clock at night. He sought to remove what he regarded as the dregs of popery and superstition, attacking plays, carnivals, and maypoles and outlawing Shrove Tuesday festivities.

In this campaign to restore righteousness, Stuyvesant made it all but oblig-atory for employees of the West India Company to regularly attend church services. In Stuyvesant's fiefdom there was to be a common day of fasting and prayer on the first Wednesday of every month. Most importantly, he was determined to counter what he regarded as the offensive plurality of New Netherlands religious life.

In theory, Stuyvesant wasn't wrong. Only the Dutch Reformed Church was entitled to public worship in New Netherland: "no other religion shall be publicly admitted . . . except the Reformed." It was quickly realized, however, that enforcing uniformity of religion would have parlous economic conse-quences. Those of other faiths, capable of bringing skills, capital, and vitality to the territory, would be alienated. And so, although the Reformed Church maintained its privileged position, a policy emerged in which the beliefs of dissenters were broadly tolerated. This appalled Stuyvesant. He found an ally in the ruling body of the Church, the Classis of Amsterdam, which also hoped to rein in the freedoms of New Netherland, as it declared in 1656: "Let us then   we here in this country and you there   employ all diligence to frustrate all such plans, that the wolves may be warded off from the tender lambs of Christ."

Say what you will, but Stuyvesant represented an influential body of opin-ion that regarded religious uniformity as eminently desirable, for social as well as theological reasons. Various dissenters, including the Baptist Wil-liam Wickenden (banished after performing adult baptisms in Long Island), incurred Stuyvesant's displeasure. Meanwhile, Lutherans in the colony had long been appealing for a right to public worship. These hopes had rou-tinely been quashed, but there was a growing tendency for members of the faith to mount private services in their homes. Even this was too much for Stuyvesant, and he pounced on the practice, issuing an ordinance in 1656 and placing some church leaders in jail. After protests, the authorities in Amsterdam ordered Stuyvesant to alter his policy, but in the coming years, the director-general seized every opportunity to harass the minority Lutheran community.

The authorities back in Amsterdam were not entirely convinced of the wisdom of Stuyvesant's approach to religious diversity. In a 1663 letter the directors of the company offered this advice:

Your last letter informed us that you had banished from the province and sent thither by ship a certain Quaker, John Bowne by name. Although we heartily desire that these and other sectarians remained away from there, yet as they do not, we doubt very much whether we can proceed against them rigorously without diminishing the population and stopping immigration, which must be favoured at so tender a stage of the country's existence.

This was Dutch pragmatism at its best. Stuyvesant was encouraged to "shut [his] eyes" and "not force people's consciences but allow everyone to have his own belief, as long as he behaves quietly and legally" and "gives no offence to his neighbours and does not oppose the government."

***

Such censures must have infuriated Stuyvesant, but there was worse to follow. Some residents in New Netherland took what they saw as the moral high ground. Enter the Quakers. Unsurprisingly, they had often suffered considerable hardship at Stuyvesant's hands. Robert Hodgson had been transported to Manhattan in a cart, and after a spell in jail, he was sentenced to hard labor. When he refused to submit, he was punished and deported to Rhode Island. In 1657, appalled by the Quaker habit of setting up private religious meetings, Stuyvesant issued an edict that introduced hefty fines for anyone found to be sheltering a Quaker in his or her home. It also ruled that any ship bringing a Quaker into the colony would be confiscated. This piece of legislation, the quintessence of state intervention in private religious belief, caused outrage in Flushing, a town with a venerable dissenting history.

The town's clerk, Edward Hart, composed a remonstrance in December 1657, and it was delivered to Stuyvesant by Tobias Feake. It has been often been identified as one of the earliest and most significant expressions of American commitment to religious toleration. "You have been pleased to send up unto us," the remonstrance began, "a certain prohibition or command that we should not receive or entertain any of those people called Quakers because they are supposed to be by some seducers of the people." The people of Flushing did not concur. "For our part we cannot condemn them in this case, neither can we stretch out our hands against them, to punish, banish or persecute them." To do so would be to risk divine displeasure. They sought, therefore, "not to judge lest we be judged, neither to condemn lest we be condemned, but rather let every man stand and fall to his own master."

There was an overriding duty, the remonstrance continued, to do "good unto all men, especially to those of the household of faith." It might seem that they were flouting the authority of the law and the law-giver by voicing their protest, but at heart, they said, this was a "case of conscience betwixt God and our own souls." It provoked decisions beyond the competence of "the powers of this world."

Once again, we should not rush to the conclusion that the residents of Flushing were motivated by modern-day notions of religious freedom. They were more concerned with denouncing an avoidable injustice. They did not quite see why the Quakers were such a threat to public order. The "jealousies and suspicions which some have of them, that they are destructive unto magistracy and ministry," were surely exaggerated. The magistrate had his sword, just as Moses had his, and the Church had its sword, just as Christ did. These institutions had been raised up by God against "all the enemies both of flesh and spirit," and those things that were of God would prevail, and those things that were "of man will come to nothing."

One only had to look to the policy of the home country for instruction and inspiration. "The law of love, peace and liberty in the states [extends] to Jews, Turks, and Egyptians, as they are considered the sons of Adam." This was "the glory of the outward state of Holland," where love, peace, and liberty had supplanted hatred, war, and bondage. Flushing had no intention of persecuting anyone who claimed to belong to Christ: "our desire is not to offend one of his little ones, in whatsoever form, name or title he appears in, whether Presbyterian, Independent, Baptist or Quaker." They were happy to "see anything of God" that was in any of them and to "do unto all men as we desire all men should doe unto us." Therefore, "if any of these said persons come in love unto us, we cannot in conscience lay violent hands upon them, but give them free egress and regress unto our town, and houses, as God shall persuade our consciences. And in this we are true subjects both of church and state, for we are bound by the law of God and man to do good unto all men and evil to no man."

Stuyvesant fell into paroxysms of anger upon receiving the remonstrance, and by early January 1658, various officials from Flushing had been arrested. What his actions could not blot out was a phenomenon that posed a major challenge to accepted ideas about Church–State relations. A town in New Netherland had simply refused to let its political masters dictate the way in which they responded to religious diversity,

The Flushing protest came and went, but another 17th-challenge would prove to be more enduring. It required the founding of a whole new colony: Pennsylvania. Once again, the Quakers would play a starring role.

## PENNSYLVANIA

The Society of Friends, better known as the Quakers, caused uproar during the 17th century. They flatly rejected established modes and methods of worship. Instead of attending services in traditional parish churches, with all the attendant sermons, salaried ministers, and rituals, they came together at silent meetings and waited patiently for Christ's voice to speak from within. This was troubling for the syndics of orthodoxy for two reasons: first, such meetings were regarded as unregulated, illegal assemblies that undermined the ecclesiastical status quo; second, they seemed to challenge established ways of worshipping God—instead of following prescribed liturgies and respecting the authority of an elevated priestly caste, the Quakers relied on the notion of the inner light and the belief that each individual could experience the immediate presence of God (the only authentic source of religious truth) through his or her own inner spirit.

The Quakers were seen as both theologically mischievous (arguing that salvation was available to all and that no one was inevitably destined for eternal perdition) and socially disruptive. Quakers were pacifists who refused to perform military service, they opposed tithes and the taking of oaths, and they strove for unprecedented levels of social equality. They rebelled against accepted social conventions such as the doffing of hats to superiors, and with scant regard for differences in social rank, they addressed everyone with familiar words such as *thee* and *thou*. What was more, the Quakers endeavored to spread these radical ideas with unbridled missionary zeal.

From the middle decades of the 17th century, the Society of Friends was denounced, often with extraordinary venom, on both sides of the Atlantic Ocean. This was an era replete with many novel dissenting groups, but none of them attracted quite so much opprobrium as the Quakers. By 1680, 10,000 of them had endured spells in English prisons—243 had died there.

The Quakers urgently required a champion, and they found one in William Penn. From the late 1660s onward, Penn would defend the tenets of Quakerism against a growing chorus of disapproval. He had his own share of spells in prison, and during one of them (between 1669 and 1670), he began work on perhaps his most treasured tract, *The Great Case of Liberty of Conscience*. In tandem with his other writings, this marked a major turning point in attitudes toward both religious freedom and the relationship between Church and State.

Penn did not simply argue from pragmatism: he defended the Quakers' right to worship as a matter of principle. He pointed to the long English tradition of liberty, dating back to Magna Carta and beyond, and insisted that Quakers, just like everyone else, were entitled to the "possession of those freedoms to which we are entitled by English birthright." The endless persecution of Quakers, the "unspeakable pressure of nasty prisons," the confiscation of goods, and the ruin of entire families was a betrayal of this luminous tradition.

In his writings Penn also made a crucial point about the true nature of freedom of conscience. He once wrote, "We understand not only a mere liberty of the mind, in believing . . . this or that principle or doctrine, but the exercise of ourselves in a visible way of worship." This was about far more than splitting hairs. A person had to be allowed to act as his beliefs required. An ability to simply think as one saw fit was not sufficient. Those who denied this idea, who persecuted their religious enemies, were poor theologians. Here we get an echo of Roger Williams. There was no point in forcing people to worship in a particular way because, owing to the nature of religious sentiment, coercion had never managed to make anyone truly believe anything. At best it served only to produce hypocrites—people who, out of fear, dutifully attended church services that they actually detested. Only God could influence the consciences of men, and "we say that the restraint and persecution for matters relating to conscience directly invade the divine right, and rob the Almighty of that which belongs to none but himself."

Penn would spill much ink pleading the case for religious toleration and arguing for a return to the verities of the "good old admirable laws of England." He would rebuke Protestants for behaving with the kind of cruelty usually associated with Catholics and for failing to see the difference between fundamental, inalterable laws and temporary laws, which were always subject to the whims of fashion. Penn suggested that in any society, there were many secondary, superficial laws, and it was entirely appropriate that a body such as Parliament should codify them. That was the rightful and righteous duty of the state. But there were also fundamental laws, grounded in the direct authority of the people, and any Parliament that became entangled with them was wholly in error.

Religious belief, for instance, was a thing with which Parliament should never meddle; there should be no established, state-sponsored religion, and even if such a religion existed, it was not appropriate to punish those who failed to follow its rubrics. For Penn, it was absurd to suggest that every subject should be compelled to attend the services of a particular sect or to financially support that sect through the payment of tithes. This last point was especially important to Penn because he saw an established Church, with the fines it imposed on nonconformists, as a threat to an Englishman's most precious privilege—the right to hold property.

Penn, as we've seen, based his entire defense of religious liberty in English tradition. During the early part of his career, he dedicated himself to helping his fellow English Quakers: paying their fines, arguing in their corner in legal proceedings, and so on. Ultimately, however, his greatest contribution to the debate about Church and State would unfold in the Americas. He would found Pennsylvania.

***

Life in England had not been easy for the Quakers. Life in the American colonies was often just as awkward. We have already seen Stuyvesant's anti-Quaker fulminations in New Netherland, but they were far from being exceptional. In 1656, when the Quakers Mary Fisher and Ann Austin arrived in Boston Harbor, they were searched for witchcraft paraphernalia, their goods were confiscated, and the two women were sent back to Barbados. They avoided more severe punishment because the local authorities lacked suitable legislation with which to prosecute them. The gap was soon plugged. The Massachusetts General Court made it illegal for Quakers to set foot in the colony. Anyone breaching this new ordinance was to be imprisoned, whipped, and deported. The mere act of helping Quakers visit the colony, or assisting them once they had arrived, would now incur hefty legal fines. By 1658, any Quaker foolish enough to return to the colony after previously being exiled would risk the death penalty, as was the fate, in 1659 and 1661, of William Robinson, William Leddra, Marmaduke Stephenson, and perhaps most famously, Mary Dyer.

These were tough colonial beginnings for the Quakers, but largely thanks to William Penn, much happier times awaited the Society of Friends elsewhere on America's eastern seaboard. Penn's interest in the American colonies had been stirred as early as 1675, when he served as mediator in a land dispute in New Jersey. Subsequent to this, Penn helped to compose some of West New Jersey's foundational documents. Amid a great deal of legalese, there was one article that delighted Penn's Quaker confreres: it allowed them to go about their religious devotions without fear of molestation:

No men, nor number of men upon earth, has power or authority to rule over men's consciences in religious matters, therefore it is consented, agreed and ordained, that no person or persons whatsoever within the said province, at any time or times hereafter, shall be any ways upon any presence whatsoever, called in question, or in the least punished or hurt, either in person, estate, or privilege, for the sake of his opinion, judgement, faith or worship towards God in matters of religion. But that all and every such person, and persons may from time to time, and at all times, freely and fully have, and enjoy his and their judgements, and the exercises of their consciences in matters of religious worship throughout all the said province.

Better was to follow.

Penn was a man of privilege: well born, well connected, and handsomely propertied. Unfortunately, his constant efforts to bail out fellow Quakers had taken their toll on his pocketbook. Most of Penn's fiscal troubles could have been easily resolved if the English king, Charles II, had settled a £16,000 debt owed to Penn's father. This, Charles was unable or unwilling to do, but as recompense, in March 1681, he granted Penn a charter for lands to the north of Maryland.

It was these sprawling territories that soon became the colony of Pennsylvania, and from the outset, Penn was determined to enshrine his religious vision in its founding documents. As the colony's "Frame of Government" explained in 1682,

all persons living in this province, who confess and acknowledge the one almighty and eternal God, to be the creator, upholder and ruler of the world; and that hold themselves obliged in conscience to live peaceably and justly in civil society, shall, in no ways, be molested or prejudiced for their religious persuasion, or practice, in matters of faith and worship, nor shall they be compelled, at any time, to frequent or maintain any religious worship, place or ministry whatever.

Pennsylvania was not the happiest of colonial experiments for its founder. Over the coming decades Penn was plagued by border disputes with Maryland, by the stirrings of internal dissent, and by a growing realization that the colony was costing him a fortune. Penn himself endured a lamentable later life, becoming increasingly ill, impoverished, and disenchanted. For all that, the colony he founded quickly became a famous refuge for those of more exotic religious sympathies. Mennonites, Moravians and Schwenkfelders, Dutch Calvinists, and German Pietists seized upon the promise of toleration and the certainty that the colony's government would not impose its authority on the ways in which they chose to worship. By as early as 1685, 8,000 people had settled in the colony, and Philadelphia, the city at the junction of the Delaware and the Schuykill, was already home to 357 households.

It would be wrong to romanticize Pennsylvania as a libertarian paradise. So far as sustaining public order was concerned, the Frame of Government made clear the government's duty to "terrify evil-doers." As Penn had always argued, human, positive law had a role in stymieing crime and immorality. Imposing a preferred vision of public morality was another of the government's most urgent tasks. The legal obstacles to activities such as card- and dice-playing, theater, and cockfighting were considerable. Nor was there total religious freedom. If you happened to be a polytheist, you would have to seek out some other oasis, and if you wanted to vote or hold public office in the colony, you still had to be a Christian. At no time did Penn seek to eliminate government's role in promoting Christian morality, and the "Great Law of Pennsylvania" of 1682 spent several sentences iterating the value of seemly Sabbath observance: on "every first day of the week, called the Lord's Day, people shall abstain from their common toil and labor, that whether masters, parents, children, or servants, they may the better dispose themselves to read the Scriptures of truth at home, or to frequent such meetings of religious worship abroad as may best suit their respective persuasions."

So far as history was concerned, however, it was the religious legacy of the Pennsylvania experiment that always seemed most epochal. All believers in one God enjoyed freedom of worship, and in the decades after Penn's death, his colony, and the city of Philadelphia most of all, would enhance its reputation as a religious sanctuary, most especially among the dissenting populations of England, Germany, Holland, and Scandinavia. By the middle of the 18th century, the colony was home to a dazzling array of competing sects and theologies, from Mennonites to Seventh-Day Baptists, from Rosicrucians to the Amish, and by 1750 Quakers represented only a quarter of the population.

Pennsylvania began life as a Quaker fiefdom. It was a place where the old, state-ordained laws of England were no longer operative and a place specifically designed to allow Quakers to worship as they chose. Within half a century, however, Quaker dominance had evaporated. Before too long Philadelphia would turn out to be the place where the Protestant Episcopal Church was constituted and the city in which the African Methodist Episcopal Church had its origins. These were the fruits of perhaps the boldest experiment in toleration that the 17th-century American colonies produced.

## SUGGESTED READING

On Roger Williams, see James Calvin Davis, *The Moral Theology of Roger Williams* (Louisville, KY, 2004); Edwin S. Gaustad, *Liberty of Conscience: Roger Williams in America* (Grand Rapids, MI, 1991); Timothy Hall, *Separating Church and State: Roger Williams and Religious Liberty* (Champaign, IL, 1998); Edmund S. Morgan, *Roger Williams: The Church and the State* (New York, 1967).

On Anne Hutchinson, see David Hall, *The Antinomian Controversy 1636–1638: A Documentary History* (Durham, NC, 1968); Amy Lang, *Prophetic Woman, Anne Hutchinson and the Problem of Dissent in the Literature of New England* (Berkeley, CA, 1987); Michael P. Winship, *Making Heretics: Militant Protestantism and Free Grace in Massachusetts, 1636–1641* (Princeton, NJ, 2002); Michael P. Winship, *The Times and Trials of Anne Hutchinson: Puritans Divided* (Lawrence, KS, 2005)

On 17th-century New England in general, see Charles Cohen, *God's Caress: The Psychology of Puritan Religious Experience* (New York, 1986); Joseph A. Conforti, *Saints and Strangers: New England in British North America* (Baltimore, 2006); Janice Knight, *Orthodoxies in Massachusetts: Rereading American Puritanism* (Cambridge, MA, 1994); David A. Weir, *Early New England: A Covenanted Society* (Grand Rapids, MI, 2005).

For Virginia and Anglicanism, see James B. Bell, *The Imperial Origins of the King's Church in Early America, 1607–1783* (London, 2004); John Frederick Woolverton, *Colonial Anglicanism in North America* (Detroit, MI, 1984). For Maryland, see John D. Krugler, *English and Catholic: The Lords Baltimore in the Seventeenth Century* (Baltimore, 2004). And for Stuyvesant and New Netherland, see Oliver Rink, *Holland on the Hudson: An Economic and Social History of Dutch New York* (Ithaca, NY, 1996). Information on the Dutch context can be found in R. Po-chia Hsia and Henk van Nierop, *Calvinism and Religious Toleration in the Dutch Golden Age* (Cambridge, UK, 2002).

On the Quakers in general, see Pink Dandelion, *An Introduction to Quakerism* (New York, 2007); and Thomas D. Hamm, *The Quakers in America* (New York, 2003). For Penn and Pennsylvania, see Hugh Barbour, ed., *William Penn on Religion and Ethics* (Lewiston, NY, 1991); William Frost, *A Perfect Freedom: Religious Liberty in Pennsylvania* (New York, 1990); Sally Schwartz, *"A Mixed Multitude": The Struggle for Toleration in Colonial Pennsylvania* (New York, 1987).

# 3

# 18th-Century Discontent

When considering William Penn, it is legitimate to identify the beginnings of a more philosophically motivated defense of religious freedom and all the consequences for Church–State debates that would be carried in its wake. As Penn happily admitted, his colonial adventures were partly motivated by the pursuit of profit and the desire to let Quakers escape persecution back in England. There was more to the Pennsylvanian enterprise than this, however. There was also a robust theoretical bedrock. By insisting that coercion in matters of faith was a futile pursuit and by grounding his arguments in a positive defence of liberty of conscience, Penn was a genuine harbinger of ideas that gained considerable support during the 18th century.

This book's introduction warned against conflating the worldviews of different historical eras, but Penn allows us to bend these rules. He was that most unusual of individuals: he stood on the cusp between ideas that had been regnant ever since Constantine and Augustine and notions that would gain increasing support in the decades and centuries following his death. Debates about Church and State would never be quite the same again.

## MAKING THINGS NEW

Previously, toleration had almost always been seen as a matter of pragmatism. Back in post-Reformation Europe, for instance, many states and cities had grown weary of the chaos and carnage produced by the era's confessional strife. It was patently clear that Protestantism was there to stay, and it had made good sense for polities to seek out compromises—some method by which those of competing confessional allegiances could coexist. Thus it was that places such as the Dutch Republic, France (at least until the revocation of the Edict of Nantes in 1685), the Polish-Lithuanian state, and any number of German towns and principalities had extended a limited tolerance to those of minority faiths.

It is crucial to recognize, however, that this was all a long way from modern conceptions of religious liberty. Even in 17th-century Holland (the poster boy of advanced 17th-century toleration), allowing Jews, Lutherans, and Catholics to go relatively unmolested was more about allowing them to contribute to the cultural, intellectual, and economic ferment of the nation than it was about countenancing their religious ideas. Similarly, moves toward toleration across the European continent were usually derived from a desire to limit the amount of inter-religious conflict and to let social and political life carry on without too many disruptions.

This pragmatic basis of toleration would never vanish. It could even be argued that it still plays an important role in motivating present-day quests for religious freedom: behind the lofty talk of ecumenism and the wonders of pluralism, there is perhaps a firm sense that avoiding inter-religious competition and sectarian hatred is the very best reason for allowing individuals to believe whatever they choose and to keep governments out of their decision-making.

For all this, it is hard to deny that that, at some indeterminate point in the 17th or 18th century, Europe—and by extension, the New World, the American colonies included—underwent something of a paradigm shift in its approach to religious diversity and its attitudes toward Church–State relationships. William Penn was clearly part of this process, as were a host of European intellectuals (many of them Dutch—and this was no coincidence). What started out as pragmatism ended up as principle. By the end of the 17th century, people such as the British philosopher John Locke were talking about a positive *right* to liberty of conscience.

This was new. The key notion was *rights*. For perhaps the very first time in the Western intellectual tradition, it was suggested that such toleration (in a far more generous sense) was worthwhile *in and of itself*. Toleration was no longer simply about containing potential chaos; it was seen as the only reputable option. Such an idea attracted many gainsayers, and codifying this novel approach was beset with difficulties, but its arrival was undoubtedly an epochal moment.

In Locke's case this liberty of conscience was limited: in the interests of social and political order he continued to insist that legal disadvantages should be applied to atheists and Catholics. That said, he made a major contribution to Western intellectual history. He suggested that although a government was perfectly entitled to supervise the worldly affairs of its subjects, it should perhaps be rather less interventionist when it came to matters of faith and conscience. Needless to say, such meditations would have profound repercussions for the issue of Church–State relations.

Writing in 1688, the English philosopher had this to say on the subject:

The commonwealth seems to me to be a society of men constituted only for the procuring, preserving, and advancing their own civil interests . . . Civil interests I call life, liberty, health . . . and the possession of outward things, such as money, lands, houses, furniture and the like.

The magistrate was entitled (duty-bound, in fact) to enforce laws that allowed his subjects to pursue such interests. Those who threatened such endeavors were to be punished, but that was as far as the magistrate's reach extended. Under no circumstances ought it "in any manner . . . be extended to the salvation of souls." God had never granted any "authority to one man over another" in matters of religion. "All the life and power of true religion consist in the inward and full persuasion" of the mind, and religion was about faith, not coercion. "The care of souls cannot belong to the civil magistrate because his power consists only in outward force; but true and saving religion consists in the inward persuasion of the mind." The similarity to some of William Penn's ideas is immediately apparent here.

These new ideas about toleration would have considerable appeal in 18th-century America, and they captured the imaginations of some of the era's brightest minds, culminating in the musings of men such as Thomas Jefferson and James Madison. Of course, others pursued a tolerationist agenda for more mundane, more familiar reasons. As numerous Americans pointed out, there was an increasingly diverse devotional climate in the colonies, with groups such as the Baptists, the Quakers, and the Methodists gaining ground and congregations with every passing decade. There was no better way of responding to this state of affairs than extending limited religious freedom to energetic and increasingly popular minority denominations.

Needless to say, many Americans were horrified by such trends, and they fought an energetic rearguard action, shoring up the privileges of established churches. Others sought to confront and cope with the new landscape. Some of them (not least members of the newer denominations themselves) embraced the centrifugal tendencies of American religious life as a positive development; for such people, the intricate philosophizing of Locke and countless other theorists was a godsend. Just as often, however, the embrace of toleration was more about common sense.

Rather than reaching definitive conclusions about which source of tolerationist thought was most important in 18th-century America—philosophical commitment or old-fashioned pragmatism—it is more sensible to see both ideas living side by side, often, it might be added, in the mindset of a single individual. Madison, for example, was driven by both a principled belief in religious freedom and a keen political sense that continuing down the route of state-sponsored, exclusivist churches could lead only to strife and division.

In any event, the 18th century would witness an extraordinary commitment to analyzing the relationship between Church and State. This would culminate in the majestic pronouncements of the First Amendment. Ahead of that, however, there were still many battles to be fought.

## TROUBLES ON THE HUDSON

New York has always played an important role in the history of Church–State relations in America. We have already seen how, under Dutch rule, there were some notable battles between the rulers and subjects of New Netherland (see chapter 2). The waters were similarly turbulent in the decades after 1664, when the English took over the colony. The newly installed Anglican Church worked tirelessly to establish itself as the colony's dominant religious power. This was part and parcel of the general effort to "anglicanize" the colony; other tactics included the introduction of English common law, English legal institutions, and English educational standards.

On the religious front, the Anglican leadership was determined to replicate the Church–State relationship that was operative back home. In many ways, this was a repeat performance of the ecclesiastical arrangements aspired to in Virginia. In 1693 the Ministry Act arrived, and funds raised from provincial taxes were now to be directed toward the support of Anglican clergy in New York, Richmond, Queens, and Winchester counties. Two years later, the colonial governor approved the granting of lands for an Anglican church, which materialized as Trinity Church in 1697.

The truculent William Vesey was its first rector, and for the next five decades, he would do a good job of epitomizing the quest for Anglican dominance in the colony. The Anglican Church's estimable privileges were to be jealously guarded, and the incursions of rival sects were to be stymied at every opportunity. For someone like Vesey, New York was to be a model of Anglicanism overseas: a dream that seemed to come a little closer in 1710 when William Bradford printed the *Book of Common Prayer, and Administration of the Sacraments*, the very first American edition of the Church of England's prayer book.

In truth, the dream was always something of a pipe dream. Relations between Anglican clerics and the colonial legislature were rarely untroubled, and non-Anglican groups (growing in strength with every passing decade) were far from pleased with the imposition of an unyielding Anglican establishment. Nonetheless, some New York politicians tried extremely hard to sustain an intimate relationship between secular and religious authority and to exhibit an unflinchingly intolerant attitude toward those of non-Anglican sympathies.

The most virulent gubernatorial opponent of dissenting religious groups was undoubtedly Edward Hyde, Lord Cornbury. Cornbury was dedicated to harassing members of other faiths and even found time to assault Dutch Reformed congregations, regardless of the fact that they had received specific promises of toleration as part of the transfer of governance from Holland to England. Anglican clerics were appointed to Dutch churches, and any number of ministers who arrived from Holland were refused preaching licenses.

Cornbury was even less enamored of Presbyterianism (just the sort of minority Protestant denomination that made a mockery of the dream of Anglican plenitude). When one of its number, Francis Makemie, started preaching around the colony, he was swiftly arrested for evangelizing without a license. Makemie knew his rights and claimed protection under the English Declaration of Religious Toleration of 1689: this was the piece of legislation that had extended various freedoms to dissenting Protestant sects in the wake of England's Glorious Revolution.

The law was self-evidently on Makemie's side: legal sanctions that applied to England were certainly intended to apply to its overseas colonies, New York included. But Cornbury simply shrugged his shoulders and claimed that the 1689 act was inapplicable in New York. He would deal with dissenters as he saw fit. After Makemie had spent 46 days in jail, the matter came to trial, and Cornbury reiterated his curious argument that, in general, laws passed in England were operative in the colonies but that such was not the case in this particular instance. The judge directed the jury to find against Makemie, but very unusually, the jurors ignored his advice and acquitted the defendant (although Makemie was still forced to meet the costs of his trial and imprisonment).

It was a shoddy episode, and by 1708, Cornbury had been recalled to England, dogged not only by talk of his gubernatorial misrule but also by rumors of his alleged transvestitism. Ludicrous as he was, it would be a mistake to see Cornbury as nothing more than an aberration. In his heavy-handed way he represented (albeit in an exaggerated, politically misguided manner) the determination to impose Anglican uniformity and conformity on New York.

The trouble was, New York was too religiously diverse for such a project to be pursued without provoking an enormous amount of dissent. There were always rival sources of religious influence in New York. The Dutch had been cast out politically, but there were still many members of the Dutch Reformed

Church, and despite Cornbury's best efforts, they endured. There were many notable pockets of dissent, perhaps most famously Jamaica parish in Queens County, which, with its largely Presbyterian population, stood out against Anglican domination, refused to pay the salary of an Anglican minister, and even resorted to rioting in 1704.

Whenever the Anglican establishment tried too hard to impose its exclusivist vision, there were sure to be protests. During the 1750s, the issue at hand (one that would come to haunt American Church–State relations) was the intersection between religion and public education.

***

In October 1754, King's College in New York City—the institution that would become Columbia University—secured its founding charter from George II. This was a major victory for the Anglican establishment because King's, the fifth of nine colleges established in colonial America (preceded by Harvard, William and Mary, Yale, and Princeton), was perceived by some New Yorkers as a solidly Anglican undertaking.

Ahead of its founding, however, a major campaign had been waged against the notion of this publicly funded Anglican-run educational institution. William Livingston, a native of Albany and a Yale alumnus, had been in the vanguard of the protest. He had succeeded in mobilizing public opinion and had made one of the most significant American contributions to the continuing debate over the troubled relationship between religions and education.

As we have seen, by the time of the King's College controversy, the Anglican establishment had demonstrated its commitment to dominating the religious life of New York. An Anglican-run college was an ideal way to pursue this objective. In October 1746, New York's General Assembly authorized a public lottery to raise £2250 "for the advancement of learning and toward the founding of a college." At this early stage it was far from inevitable that the new college would be run by the Anglican Church. There was no mention of this in the Assembly's proceedings, and Livingston himself had no objection, in principle, to New York setting up dynamic educational institution; more than that, he even devoted some of his time to raising funds for the venture.

It quickly became apparent, however, that the Anglican establishment, both in New York and back in England, was determined to secure leadership over the proposed college. This became abundantly clear when William Smith published his *Some Thoughts on Education: With Reasons for Erecting a College in This Province,* in which he proposed that the college be Anglican-controlled, adding a short time later that the ideal candidate for the post of president was the Anglican cleric Samuel Johnson.

For Livingston, this was a transparent example of Church and State in cahoots, and his attitude toward the proposed college changed dramatically. In six issues of the *Independent Reflector,* dating from March 1753 onward, he mounted an assault on the prospect of an Anglican-dominated college. He articulated just the sorts of concerns mentioned earlier. He asked a fundamental question: was there really a place for such an institution, supported at least in part by public funds, in a religiously mixed city (brimful of Presbyterians, Lutherans, Quakers, Dutch Calvinists, Anabaptists, and Moravians) where Anglicans represented only something like 15 percent of the population?

Livingston stressed his passionate belief in providing a good education for the city's youth. "Erecting a college in this province is a matter of such grand and general importance," he explained, "that I have frequently made it the topic of my serious meditation." It was a "subject of universal concernment" and of the greatest "importance to the happiness and well-being of our posterity." Everyone had agreed that a college should certainly be within, or very close to, the city, but so much time had been spent mulling over its precise location that the issues of the college's governance and constitution had been neglected.

Livingston embraced the laudable aims of such an institution. Students were to be sent there to "improve their hearts and understandings, to infuse a public spirit and love of their country." They were to be inspired with "the principles of honour and probity; with a fervent zeal for liberty, and a diffusive benevolence for mankind." In this way they would be made "the more extensively serviceable to the commonwealth." Who could question such noble aspirations? But this made it all the more important that such a college be set up on the most equitable and progressive basis possible.

"The necessity and importance of constituting our college upon a basis the most catholic, generous and free" was paramount. Allowing one religious group to dominate would be disastrous. It would immediately exclude huge swathes of the city's population, and this could not possibly be of general benefit to New York. Instead, it was crucial to "admit persons of all Protestant denominations, upon a perfect parity as to privileges"; otherwise, "it will itself be greatly prejudiced, and prove a nursery of animosity, dissention and disorder." Here, Livingston was being pristinely pragmatic.

If King's turned out to be an Anglican undertaking, what were the likely results? There was no avoiding the fact that every person thinks his own sect to be superior and therefore strives to strengthen his own church at the expense of others. Given this, if "our college . . . unhappily through our own bad policy, fall[s] into the hands of any one religious sect in the province," then that sect would certainly "establish its religion in the college, show favour to its votaries, and cast contempt upon others." Just as inevitably, "Christians of all other denominations amongst us, instead of encouraging its prosperity, will, from the same principles, rather conspire to oppose and oppress it."

This would represent a missed opportunity. What might have been a well-spring of prosperity for the entire community would become a force for division. Anglicans would be pleased; everyone else would be angry. Whichever sect had "the sole government of the college, will kindle the jealousy of the rest, not only against the persuasion so preferred, but the college itself," and this could contribute only to a "general discontent and tumult; which, affecting all ranks of people, will naturally tend to disturb the tranquility and peace of the province."

Only the children of Anglicans would be sent there, and instead of receiving a rounded education, they would be drowned in theological "quibbles and trifles." As for the rest of the population, those blessed with good incomes would look elsewhere—doubtless outside the colony—but the rest would simply keep their children at home.

One thing should be made very clear: Livingston was not opposed to religious worship playing a role at the proposed college; on the contrary, that it "should be constantly maintained there," he said, "I am so far from opposing, that I strongly recommend it, and do not believe any such kind of society can be kept under a regular and due discipline without it." His objection was to state-sponsorship of a *specific* variety of worship and instruction.

For Livingston, a fundamental issue was at stake. It was public money that would help set up the college, and "when the community is taxed, it ought to be for the defence, or emolument of the whole . . . Can it, therefore, be supposed, that all shall contribute for the uses, the ignominious uses, of a few?" A true public academy is "or ought to be a mere civil institution, and cannot with any tolerable propriety be monopolized by any religious sect." Livingston thus wholly opposed the notion of a chartered school with authority vested in a board of sectarian trustees. The inevitable consequence was that "the civil and religious principles of the trustees, will become universally established, liberty and happiness be driven without our borders, and in their room erected the banners of spiritual and temporal bondage."

He continued, "We expect to fill our public posts with persons of wisdom and understanding, worthy of their offices," so the college should be established not by a charter, but by act of assembly. It should be open to public inspection and scrutiny, allowing the community to "counterplot every scheme that can possibly be concerted, for the advancement of any particular sect above the rest." There was to be no room for any "religious profession in particular [to] be established in the college; but that both officers and scholars be at perfect liberty to attend any Protestant Church at their pleasure respectively." The ruling body of the school was to "be absolutely inhibited" from "making of any by-laws relating to religion, except such as compel them to attend divine service at some church or other, every Sabbath."

But we should not get carried away when analyzing Livingstone's platform. He was not against the state supporting religion in an educational institution per se. On the contrary, he thought this was, if suitably constrained, a very good idea. The ideal college would have a Christian ethos; more specifically, it would have a Protestant ethos, and Christian morality was to pervade the institution. There should be public prayers and services, but—and here was the crucial point—they should be palatable to all Protestants and not just Anglicans.

Just as importantly, and here Livingston was being rather radical, the religious dimension of the college should encompass only such general acts of worship and a general commitment to instilling good, Christian verities. Beyond this, specific religious instruction was to "be no part of the public exercises of the college," and degrees in divinity were not to be offered, not least because of the "disgust which will necessarily be given to all parties" who differed in their beliefs from any particular professor. There was to be free access to books about divinity, and it was to be freely discussed, but any public disputations on particular matters of faith were to be forbidden.

Livingston believed that fundamental principles were at stake, and basic freedoms were under threat:

Arise, therefore, and baffle the machinations of your and their country's foes. Every man of virtue, every man of honour, will join you in defeating so iniquitous a design. To overthrow it, nothing is wanting but your own resolution. For great is the authority, exalted the dignity, and powerful the majesty of the people. And shall you the avowed enemies of usurpation and tyranny,—shall you, the descendants of *Britain*, born in a land of light, and reared in the bosom of liberty,—shall you commence cowards at a time when reason calls so loud for your magnanimity? I know you scorn such an injurious aspersion. I know you disdain the thoughts of so opprobrious a servility; and what is more, I am confident the moment you exert a becoming fortitude, they will be shamed out of their insolence.

Livingston knew his audience, and he ended his appeal by challenging each of New York's non-Anglican groups to cherish and defend their own heritage. The Dutch, he suggested, ought to reflect on the "zeal of your ancestors," and the Presbyterians should "remember with a sacred jealousy, the countless sufferings of your pious predecessors, for liberty of conscience, and the right of private judgment." What afflictions "did they not endure, what fiery trials did they not encounter," before they had found in America "that sanctuary and requiem which their native soil inhumanly denied them?" As for the Quakers, he said they had always considered themselves "lovers of civil and religious liberty," and although they had been "misrepresented as averse to human learning," Livingston remained confident that they would "generously contribute to the support of a college founded on a free and catholic bottom." At heart, Livingston was arguing that the diversity of New York's religious landscape ought (within tell-tale Protestant limits) to be reflected in the constitution and policy of its new college, and throughout, he was determined to stymie the Anglican establishment's (most especially its London-based syndics) attempts to impose its will.

For all his pleading—and it represented some of the most inspired, undaunted journalism of the 18th century—Livingston was fighting a losing battle. It became clear that the proposed college was destined to be set up on principles with which Livingston could never agree. His cause was further hindered when, in the aftermath of the suicide of governor Sir Danvers Osborne in October 1753, Livingston's arch, proudly Anglican enemy James DeLancey was appointed to the colony's highest office. DeLancey brought financial pressure to bear, and the *Reflector* (the organ in which Livingston had vented his spleen) was forced to close.

Worse yet, and largely in response to Livingston's attacks in the press, the vestrymen of Trinity Church applied two conditions to their provision of the land on which the college was to be built. In May 1754 they demanded that the college's president always be an Anglican and that services in the college always be conducted according to the rites of the Church of England. Here, very obviously, was the Anglican establishment asserting itself. A furious Livingston made a final, if rather repetitious, stand. First, he argued, in New York, "all his majesty's Protestant subjects inhabiting the same are with respect to the enjoyment of their religion, on a perfect equality; and therefore the said establishment will be partial, a manifest encroachment on the rights and privileges of all different denominations of Christians residing in the province." Second, there was a gross injustice in the fact that "all the inhabitants of the province will be obliged to contribute to its support" because "a vast majority of the province are Protestants dissenting from the Church of England." Third, it was surely unjust that the charter "excludes from the office of president all persons whatsoever who are not of the Church of England": this "not only tends to raise animosities among the good people of this colony, by introducing a discrimination of privileges, and establishing a superiority among the different sects of Christians hitherto unknown among us, but is also likely to prove prejudicial to the education of the youth to be brought up" in the college.

Livingston lost the fight. The vestrymen's conditions were accepted, and the first students arrived in July 1754. In the long term, however, the whirligig of history brought its revenges. King's College developed along lines rather different from those intended by its founders. Ultimately, all New Yorkers would be eligible to attend, and by the time of the revolution, its Anglican identity was all but a dead letter. Just as importantly, Livingston had launched a powerful assault that had portrayed the Anglican establishment as a likely enemy of American freedoms. As relations soured between London and the colonies in the coming years, this was a theme to which Livingston would return with gusto.

William Livingston is not nearly as well-remembered as he should be. He was not, absolutely not, a forerunner of modern-day critics of state support for religious educational institutions. Livingston believed passionately in the importance of Christian morality, and his preferred version of King's College would have had Christianity in its bones. More than that, he was determined that Protestant Christianity should be regnant. He was not an advocate of unregulated religious freedom; after all, he was none too impressed by Christians of non-Protestant persuasions.

What he did argue, however, was that state support for a specific Protestant denomination was sometimes a recipe for disaster. This was a battle to which he returned. The King's College controversy was not to be Livingston's last tussle with the Anglican establishment. As has already been mentioned, there was always a glaring gap in colonial ecclesiastical arrangements. It had long been argued in some quarters that Anglican-leaning colonies were in desperate need of their own bishop, and in 1767 Thomas Bradbury Chandler produced his *Appeal to the Public,* in which he articulated various arguments for sending a bishop across the Atlantic. Most importantly, he suggested, it was plainly impossible for the Church to carry out its duties without an episcopal presence—not least when it came to ordaining new clerics. He argued that preventing the Church from having its own bishop was, in fact, a denial of its religious freedoms, and he sought to reassure his critics by promising that a bishop would neither indulge in persecutory behavior nor necessarily be an unwelcome drain on public funds.

Such proposals caused considerable alarm, not least because this was a time when Anglicanism was becoming increasingly linked in the public imagination with the unpopular activities of the British monarchy. Livingston was one of many who militated against the notion of introduction of an Anglican bishop. Indeed, it was during these years that he emerged as one of the most passionate critics of the colonial policies issuing from London—policies that, very often, were supported by the very Anglican clergy with whom Livingston quarreled. Suddenly, the campaign to combat the dominance of a London-centric elite had become even more urgent.

It is therefore very easy to see Livingston as a harbinger of future ideas about Church and State. In some, albeit vague, ways he was, and it is impossible to ignore his clarion call, published in the *New Jersey Gazette* in February 1778: "the consciences of men," he wrote, "are not the object of human legislation."

We should still be cautious about recruiting Livingston as a separationist *avant la lettre*, however. He demanded change, but the limits of that change would not have measured up to modern-day expectations. The same could be said of another group that worked hard during the 18th century to transform America's attitude toward the interplay between faith and politics: the Baptists.

## BAPTIST COMPLAINTS

One thing was now becoming abundantly clear. American Protestantism was an extraordinarily diverse phenomenon, and members of disadvantaged denominations (alongside those, like Livingston, who appreciated the sense of cultural flux) were more than capable of launching their protests against the ecclesiastical status quo. The old vision of a single Protestant group enjoying unfettered access to state support was destined to come under increasing scrutiny during the 18th century. Unsurprisingly, it was the members of vibrant but still marginalized groups who often led the charge.

In truth, there had been no avoiding the power of dissenting Protestantism ever since the phenomenon known to history as the Great Awakening. Recent scholarship has reminded us that talking about a coherent, easily defined Great Awakening movement is wrongheaded. Pinning down its chronology, its aims, or its geographical reach is enormously difficult. It is far too easy to make a digestible historical construct out of endlessly diverse phenomena. For all these important correctives, it remains legitimate to suggest that something unusual and far-reaching occurred during the religious revivals of the 1730s and 1740s.

The withering critique of spiritual malaise launched by men such as the Northampton minister Jonathan Edwards and the itinerant preaching of George Whitefield, Gilbert and William Tennent, James Davenport, and Eleazar Wheelock all contributed to a transformation of America's religious landscape. It was a movement (if we are still allowed to use the term) that cut across social classes, from the slave communities that were touched by a personal religiosity as never before to the studies of New England.

In some ways, the Great Awakening was a conservative movement: for those like Edwards it was chiefly about a return to older, more rigorous standards of Calvinistic theology. At the same time, however, it was socially and theologically explosive, and it captured the imagination of a surprisingly wide swathe of the American population—including members of dissenting Protestant groups.

The champions of conservatism were eager to express their distaste for this overflowing of spontaneous religious sentiment. They complained endlessly that the frenzies being whipped up by zealous evangelists posed a serious threat to public order and common decency. Ordinary parishioners were being encouraged to question the caliber of their spiritual leaders and to embark on their own religious odysseys. Once again, the state felt obliged to intervene, as when a legislator such as Jonathan Law, governor of Connecticut, worked hard to hinder evangelical efforts by the strict enforcement of laws against itinerant preaching. Various religious leaders were equally unimpressed, and the Boston minister Charles Chauncy offered a harsh analysis of unseemly revivalist meetings characterized by people "swooning away and falling to the ground . . . bitter shriekings and screaming; convulsion-like tremblings and agitations."

This was a hard-fought polemical battle, but for all the criticism it provoked (and it certainly had its excesses), the Great Awakening brought one undeniable fact into the sharpest focus: American Protestantism was now a house divided, and dissenting groups had no intention of hiding their evangelical light under a bushel. In subsequent decades members of those denominations became increasingly vocal about their discontents. They called for a shift in the relationship between Church and State. In those places where a single denomination was privileged and supported by the state and paid for by everyone's tax dollars, regardless of individuals' religious beliefs, this proved to be a cause of great controversy.

\*\*\*

Today, Baptists make up the largest Protestant denomination in the United States. This success represents the culmination of an often troubled history. During the 17th century, Baptists were immediately treated with suspicion in the colonies of New England because of their refusal to countenance infant baptism. This doctrinal position had caused great controversy throughout the Reformation period, and by the middle of the 17th century, it was still perceived as a noxious threat to Christian tradition. Rhode Island, Pennsylvania, New Jersey, and Delaware did provide welcome refuges from persecution, but by the middle of the 18th century, the Baptists were still regarded with grave misgivings by the Christian mainstream because of their unusual theology and their radical vision of the Church.

For Baptists, as for so many other dissenting groups, the Great Awakening was of huge importance. The Awakening had a tendency to split existing congregations, with revivalist "New Lights" expressing disdain for, and often separating from, conservative "Old Lights." In New England alone, more than a hundred groups, many of them eventually adopting Baptist identity, broke away from the Congregational Church and sought, over time, to assert their religious rights. This extraordinary fragmentation represented the backdrop of Isaac Backus's religious odyssey.

Isaac Backus was born on January 9, 1724, in Norwich, Connecticut. His family had enjoyed a turbulent religious past, and there were soon signs that Isaac had inherited this passion for religious controversy.

In 1741, just as the Great Awakening was gathering steam, Backus had been mesmerized by the radical preaching of Jedediah Mills, Eleazar Wheelock, Benjamin Pomeroy and James Davenport. The results, if we are to trust Backus's account, were staggering: "As I was mowing alone in a field. . . . all my past life was open plainly before me, and I saw clearly that it had been filled up with sin." After suitable spells of prayer and meditation, the divine light revealed "the freeness and richness of grace." "My heavy burden was gone, tormenting fears were fled, and my joy was unspeakable." It was the quintessential 18th-century conversion experience.

Backus quickly became troubled by his attendance at existing religious services, not least by the prospect of worshipping alongside those who had not yet experienced a reportable moment of sanctification and conversion. Into the bargain, his local minister, Benjamin Lord, was deeply suspicious of New Light evangelism. Backus and some of his fellow parishioners began to organize meetings in the own homes (almost always the first step for potential separatists), and in the summer of 1746, they set up a separatist congregation of their own—the Bean Hill Separate Church. Backus had definitively allied himself with the New Light faction: a movement that, for the most part, was determined to exist outside of existing ecclesiastical structures.

Needless to say, such congregations were frowned on by the established churches of New England, and they endured the kinds of discriminatory treatment that would aggravate Backus throughout his career. Even though they had little sympathy for the region's state-sponsored denominations, members of the separatist congregation were still expected to pay for them, contributing the religious taxes levied in support of the established church. Backus knew all about the problems that this situation could provoke: his mother and one of his brothers refused to pay up and endured a spell in prison for their troubles. Over the next few decades, Backus would work tirelessly to remedy this parlous state of affairs.

One of the great threats of separatist congregations, at least from the perspective of the established churches, was that they rode roughshod over the concept of a tightly controlled, suitably educated ministry. The belief that unordained individuals, who often lacked college degrees, were entirely fitted for clerical duties was a hallmark Baptist belief and one to which Backus eagerly responded. After two years of itinerant sermonizing, he heard about an opening in Titicut, part of the towns of Middleborough and Bridgewater, Massachusetts. In April 1748 Backus was ordained as elder to the separatist Titicut faithful. Three years later, he and his wife went through the ceremony of adult baptism, and although Backus endeavored to dampen down divisions at Titicut between advocates and opponents of adult baptism, by 1756 it had become clear that a line had to be drawn in the sand. In that year, the First Baptist Church of Middleborough was established. Backus, now an unabashed Baptist, would serve its congregation for the next 50 years

No issue was more dear to him than the campaign to assert Baptists' rights to free exercise of their religious faith and to exclusion from the requirement to support state-backed churches whose doctrines Baptists flatly rejected. For Backus, the existing relationship was entirely untenable and a flagrant assault on Baptist consciences.

As we have already seen, the established churches of New England were supported by public taxation, and this had traditionally been collected from every member of the community, regardless of their particular religious beliefs. Some people's hard-earned dollars were thus spent on the salaries of ministers they had no intention of ever listening to and on the maintenance of churches or meeting houses into which they would never set foot. To refuse such demands was to risk imprisonment or the confiscation of property—precisely what had happened to members of Backus's own family.

This system had been subtly but significantly altered in the years ahead of Backus's arrival on the national religious scene. From 1731, Protestant dissenters in Massachusetts, provided they could demonstrate that they were genuine members of alternative congregations, could theoretically be exempted from the general religious taxes. The trouble was, and this is what so infuriated Backus, to enjoy this dispensation, individuals had to provide certificates testifying that they regularly attended religious meetings of their own and that they made financial contributions to their own churches.

This might be perceived as progress. Unfortunately, at least so far as Baptists such as Backus were concerned, there were various kinks in the execution of the law. The Massachusetts authorities were often reluctant to accept that Baptists deserved the aforementioned tax breaks, and they were routinely denied access to the tax exemption laws. This caused uproar. In 1747 Baptists complained about their inclusion in a general tax levied at Titicut to provide funds for a new Congregational meeting house. Two years later, Backus wrote to Baptists throughout Massachusetts, urging them to sign a petition that demanded the granting of the exemptions already enjoyed by Quakers and Anglicans. In 1765, Backus would petition once more in favor of the rights of Baptists in Ashfield to be freed from religious taxation.

This was all easily perceived as an attack on existing Church–State relations, and to be sure, the colony of Massachusetts was sluggish in its acceptance of Baptists as a legitimate dissenting denomination. Thus far, however, Backus had really been arguing only for a modified version of state intervention in religious affairs. From the early 1770s he began to realize that even requiring non-Congregationalists to provide a certificate that demonstrated their commitment to an alternative denomination was an imposition too far. Why should you have to convince the state that you deserved exemption from general taxation? Was this really any of the state's business? It was at this point that Backus entered the territory of principled belief in freedom of conscience. The result was a rejection of existing ideas about how Church and State ought to interact.

In 1773 Backus, always a prolific writer, composed his most memorable tract: *An Appeal to the Public for Religious Liberty*. With echoes of Williams, Locke, and Penn, he asserted that "God has appointed two kinds of government in this world . . . which are distinct in their nature, and ought never to be confounded together; one of which is called civil, the other ecclesiastical government." Christian ministers derived their authority from Christ, and they were making a fatal mistake if they looked to the state to legitimize or financially support them:

Can any man in the light of truth maintain his character as a minister of Christ, if he is not contented with all that Christ's name and influence will procure for him, but will have recourse to the *kings of the earth,* to force money from the people to support him under the name of an ambassador of the God of heaven?

Like so many champions of Church–State separation, Backus looked back to the pre-Constantine centuries when Christianity "made no use of secular force in the first setting up of the gospel church." Why, therefore, was it necessary now? Just like Penn, Williams, and Locke, Backus accepted that obedience to civil authority, in matters truly under its jurisdiction, was a vital Christian duty—"we view it to be our incumbent duty to render unto Caesar the things that are his"—but it was

of as much importance not to render unto him anything that belongs only to God, who is to be obeyed rather than man. And as it is evident to us that God always claimed it as his sole prerogative to determine, by his own laws, what his worship shall be, who shall minister in it, and how they shall be supported; so it is evident that his prerogative has been, and still is, encroached upon in our land.

The magistrates of Massachusetts, by forcing people to support a minister of particular beliefs, were betraying the authentic Christian tradition. Just as importantly, those same magistrates, by requiring the colony's citizenry to jump through hoops that proved their dissenting credentials and entitled them to tax exemptions, were straying into unwelcome territory.

Backus was becoming increasingly truculent. In the same year as his *Appeal,* he lent his support to a campaign of Baptist civil disobedience, urging his coreligionists to snub their noses at the concept of exemption certificates. What right did the civil authorities have to demand such documents? What right did civil power have to raise one sect above the other and force the citizenry to support it? Civil power had no ecclesiastical power, no right to interfere in the affairs of Christ. For the secular branch of government to raise religious taxes was abhorrent, but so, within that abhorrent system, was the process of deciding who deserved exemptions whereby people had to provide the state with written proof of their religious allegiance.

At this point, events played into Backus's hands. Revolution, which always welcomes radical theorizing, was in the air. In September 1774, "the elders and brethren of twenty Baptist churches met in association at Medfield" and sent Backus as their representative to the First Continental Congress, sitting at Philadelphia. Backus's moment had arrived, and he set about shaming the assembled delegates (who were brimful of talk of rights and freedoms) into compliance. He astutely conflated the Baptists' claims for liberty with the broader claims that were in so very much in vogue:

We would beg leave to say that, as a distinct denomination of Protestants, we conceive that we have an equal claim to charter-rights with the rest of our fellow-subjects; and yet have long been denied the free and full enjoyment of those rights, as to the support of religious worship . . . What is the liberty desired? The answer is: as the kingdom of Christ is not of this world, and religion is a concern between God and the soul, with which no human authority can intermeddle, consistently with the principles of Christianity, and according to the dictates of Protestantism, we claim and expect the liberty of worshipping God according to our consciences, not being obliged to support a ministry we cannot attend.

Perhaps surprisingly, the response to Backus's plea was less than encouraging. Casting off the English yoke was one thing; supporting Baptists was apparently quite another. Samuel Adams, for instance, readily admitted that there was an ecclesiastical establishment, but only "a very slender one, hardly to be called an establishment." The argument behind this was presumably that tax exemptions existed for those who deserved them, so why all the grumbles? Another delegate suggested that what the Baptists were complaining about was not really a matter of conscience but merely a "contending about paying a little money." The old notion that Baptists were simply tax-dodgers was still alive and well, and it provoked the bluntest of responses from Backus: "it is absolutely a point of conscience with me; for I cannot give in the certificate they require without implicitly acknowledging that power in man which I believe belongs only to God." Again, why should the state be allowed to meddle in such matters? Why should a Baptist, or anyone else, have to explain his religious preferences to secular authority?

At the end of a lengthy discussion, John Adams's conclusion was that "we might as well expect a change in the solar system as to expect they would give up their establishment." At the time, and this is an easily forgotten fact, this was probably the dominant opinion. As we'll see, John Adams would be proved wrong, but in the interim, the defeated Backus had not quite given up the fight. In December 1774 it was the Massachusetts legislature's turn to hear Backus out. His masterstroke, already hinted at in Philadelphia, was to invoke the aspirations and rhetoric of the revolution in which America was now embroiled.

It seems that the two main rights which all Americans are contending for at this day are: not to be taxed where they are not represented; and to have their causes tried by unbiased judges. And the Baptist churches in this province as heartily unite with their countrymen in this cause, as any denomination in the land; and are as ready to exert all their abilities to defend it. Yet only because they have thought it to be their duty to claim an equal title to these rights with their neighbors, they have repeatedly been accused of evil attempts against the general welfare of the colony; therefore, we have thought it expedient to lay a brief statement of the case before this assembly. . . . to impose religious taxes is as much out of [the legislature's] jurisdiction as it can be for Britain to tax America; yet how much of this has been done in this province . . . Must we be blamed for not lying still, and thus let our countrymen trample upon our rights, and deny us that very liberty that they are ready to take up arms to defend for themselves? You profess to exempt us from taxes to your worship, and yet tax us every year. Great complaints have been made about a tax which the British Parliament laid upon paper; but you require a paper tax of us annually. That which has made the greatest noise is a tax of three pence a pound upon tea; but your law of last June laid a tax of the same sum every year upon the Baptists in each parish . . . All America are alarmed at the tea tax; though, if they please, they can avoid it by not buying the tea; but we have no such liberty. . . . But these lines are to let you know, that we are determined not to pay either of them; not only upon your principle of not being taxed where we are not represented, but also because we dare not render that homage to any earthly power, which I and many of my brethren are fully convinced belongs only to God. Here, therefore, we claim charter rights, liberty of conscience.

This was genius on Backus's part. He turned the no taxation without representation rallying cry to Baptist advantage. For all that, it was a battle that Backus would never entirely win. At the Massachusetts constitutional convention in 1779, he pushed for an end to *all* religious taxation, but the state's new constitution took a slightly different tack. The state would still force each town to support (through its taxes) a Protestant minister, but the variety of minister was up for negotiation. If a township had, say, a Quaker or a Baptist majority, then those who regularly attended that town's religious services would see their tax dollars going toward the support of their own churches.

This was certainly progressive. "No subordination of any one sect or denomination shall ever be established by law," and religious pluralism was to exist alongside a mild, slender establishment. Preferred forms of Christian piety would enjoy local privileges, but individuals who subscribed to a religious belief that did not threaten morality would bask in the liberty of their consciences: they could believe whatever they chose. Thanks to this settlement, "it can no longer be called into question [that] . . . authority in magistrates and obedience of citizens can be grounded on reason, morality and the Christian religion without . . . the monkery of priests or the knavery of politicians."

Even this, so far as Backus was concerned, was an unholy sort of compromise. Civil government was still deeply embroiled in religious affairs; imposing a dozen different sort of religious tax was no better than imposing just one. The state was still there. By Backus's account, churches ought to be supported by voluntary contributions or not at all. It was not until 1833, 28 years after Backus's death, that establishment of any variety was finally banished from Massachusetts.

Ahead of this, Backus spent the remainder of his life battling against what he perceived as unnecessary Church–State interaction at the state level. The Massachusetts legal principle that no religious congregation could enjoy legal recognition (and hence tax privileges) until it had been officially incorporated caused Backus especial concern—it was the old certificate-logic in new clothes: the state was still there approving and disapproving. Unsurprisingly, because it made devotional life a good deal easier, many Baptist communities tried to secure legal incorporation from the legislature. By doing this they could ensure that the taxes they paid would be given to their chosen ministers. If incorporation was not secured, then Baptists who refused to pay religious taxes would face the risks of imprisonment or distraint of property. What was more, incorporation also ensured that ministers would receive a regular, dependable salary rather than having to rely on intermittent voluntary contributions. Many Baptists saw this as an acceptable deal.

Backus was not one of them. Such a trend continued to appall him: it was yet another example of the state exercising unwarranted authority (the gift of incorporation) in religious matters. During the 1790s Backus's counsel was sought by a group of Baptists in New Gloucester. They had only a part-time minister, and the rest of the town regarded this as insufficient grounds for granting them tax exemptions. The town suggested that they should seek incorporation from the General Court or face the consequences. Follow the rules and all will be set fair. Backus was adamant that this quest for the state's rubber stamp was an assault on their consciences. He told the Baptists of New Gloucester that they should not seek incorporation and should suffer whatever punishments might result from their refusal to pay the town's religious taxes.

***

On this issue, Backus would not budge, but as the attentive reader will have noticed, we have been getting ahead of ourselves. Backus never quite won the day in Massachusetts, but at a loftier, federal level, it is fair to say that he had the last laugh. In the wake of revolution, a whole new way of conceptualizing the encounter between religion and politics emerged. It was one with which Backus would have broadly agreed. It fell to men such as James Madison and Thomas Jefferson, and not forgetting another Baptist, John Leland, to complete the work of transforming America's attitude toward Church–State relations. Needless to say, not everyone was pleased with the results. The next two centuries, the subject of the second half of this book, were just as contested as their predecessors. This story begins, just like an earlier one, in Virginia.

## SUGGESTED READING

Important discussions of the rise of tolerationist ideas include Ole Peter Grell and Robert Scribner, *Tolerance and Intolerance in the European Reformation* (Cambridge, UK, 1996); John Marshall, *John Locke, Toleration and Early Enlightenment Culture* (Cambridge, UK, 2006); Andrew Murphy, *Conscience and Community: Revisiting Toleration and Religious Dissent in Early Modern England and America* (University Park, PA, 2001); Perez Zagorin, *How the Idea of Religious Tolerance Came to the West* (Princeton, NJ, 2003).

On Livingston and King's College, see Donald Gerardi, "The King's College Controversy 1753–56 and the Ideological Roots of Toryism in New York," *Perspectives in American History* 11 (1977–78): 145–96; David Humphrey, *From King's College to Columbia, 1754–1800* (New York, 1976); Milton M. Klein, *The American Whig: William Livingston of New York* (New York, 1993).

On the Baptists, see Bill J. Leonard, *Baptists in America* (New York, 2005); William G. McLoughlin, *Soul Liberty: The Baptists' Struggle in New England, 1630–1833* (Hanover, NH, 1991); Jewel L. Spangler, *Virginians Reborn: Anglican Monopoly, Evangelical Dissent, and the Rise of the Baptists in the Late Eighteenth Century* (Charlottesville, VA, 2008). And on Backus, see Stanley Grenz, *Isaac Backus: Puritan and Baptist* (Macon, GA, 1983); William G. McLoughlin, *Isaac Backus and the American Pietistic Tradition* (Boston, MA, 1967).

For the Great Awakening, see Thomas S. Kidd, *The Great Awakening: The Roots of Evangelical Christianity in Colonial America* (New Haven, CT, 2007).

# 4

# Jefferson and Madison

It is absolutely essential that we try to pin down exactly what Isaac Backus hoped to achieve in the realms of religious freedom and Church–State relations. He manifestly did not object to religion playing a crucial role in public life. As he once explained, Christianity was "as necessary for the well being of human society as salt is to preserve putrefaction." Backus wanted to put an end to unnecessary entanglement between State and Church not because of any antagonism toward religion but because he calculated that this was the very best way to allow religion (more precisely, the Baptist religion) to thrive. The state was not there to impinge directly on individual consciences or to make believers prove their Christian credentials (by demanding certificates of dissenting opinion or by requiring churches to secure incorporation, for example), but it still had a duty to maintain a pious devotional climate.

Backus never wanted Christianity to abandon its guiding moral role in American culture, and he was not nearly as strictly separationist as some of his more radical contemporaries. He petitioned Congress in 1791 to set up a federal commission charged with licensing the publication of Bibles, he wanted religion to permeate education in public schools, and he had no objection to the enforcement of anti-blasphemy laws. It is also worth pointing out that although he worked tirelessly to secure the rights of Baptists, he was no advocate of unbridled religious freedom. During his long career, there were moments when he had negative things to say about, among others, Universalists, Shakers, and those of Arminian tendencies.

Backus's agenda was very specific. He was determined to undermine the notion of an explicit establishment of either a single or multiple religious domination or dominations. It was this notion of direct state sponsorship and support to which he so passionately objected. The state had a role in religious matters; the problem was simply that, for Backus, it sometimes overstepped the mark.

During the turbulent revolutionary era, such opinions were shared by many other Americans. In 1777, for instance, no less than 11 separatist churches in Connecticut asked the state's legislature to grant them relief from the taxes aimed at supporting the Congregational establishment: "we though it a good time now . . . when all are earnestly contending for what they call their rights and privileges for us under this oppression to make . . . a bold claim for our just rights and privileges." In the same year, William Tennent III called for the disestablishment of South Carolina's Anglican Church. Much like Backus, he exploited the general mood of liberation. As he informed the state's assembly, there was no better time to assault the "odious discrimination" under which those of non-Anglican sympathies suffered. "Government has returned to its just and natural source and a constitution is framing with a view to perpetuate the freedom and quite of the good people of this state." At such an epochal moment, "equality or nothing ought to be our motto. In short every plan of establishment must operate as a plan of injustice and oppression and . . . [I] am utterly against all establishment in this state." It was high time for South Carolina to "yield to the mighty current of American freedom and glory."

No state in the fledgling union was more energized by such sentiments than Virginia. Here, largely thanks to the musings and machinations of Thomas Jefferson and James Madison, a fierce battle raged between those who sought to maintain some variety of religious establishment and those who wanted to erect a firm barrier between Church and State.

## JEFFERSON AND VIRGINIA

Thomas Jefferson has always been the hero of the strict separationists. This is largely due to a famous letter he wrote in 1802, during his turbulent presidential term, to the Baptists of Danbury:

Believing with you that religion is a matter which lies solely between man and his God, that he owes account to none other for his faith or his worship, that the legitimate powers of government reach actions only, I contemplate with sovereign reverence that act of the whole American people which declared that their legislature should "make no law respecting an establishment of religion or prohibiting the free exercise thereof," thus building a wall of separation between church and state.

The "act of the whole American people" to which Jefferson was referring was, of course, the First Amendment, and as this chapter continues, we see how this famous document came into being. Long before that, however, Jefferson had been campaigning for a radical recasting of America's attitude toward Church–State relations. The Danbury letter undoubtedly summed up Jefferson's attitude: at the level of legislation, he wanted the state to have very little to do with the policing of religious belief. It is important to stress, however, that this did not make Jefferson a modern secularist or a sworn enemy of Christianity.

Interpreting Jefferson accurately is very important for any nuanced understanding of America's debate about Church and State. His is the name invoked (either positively or negatively) more than any other, so we need to get him right. His actual intentions and desires (as opposed to their caricatured misrepresentations) were first revealed long before the arrival of the First Amendment or the Danbury letter. His quest began in his home state of Virginia.

***

Jefferson's religious identity is infuriatingly difficult to define. In some ways he was a classic 18th-century Deist. Deism did not deny the existence of God: rather, it suggested that although He had set the universe in motion at the beginning of time, God was no longer intervening directly in human affairs. He was not the divine character, so beloved of much orthodox Christianity, who listened to prayers or punished mankind via plague and pestilence. One of the consequences of this idea was that the superstitious rituals of organized religion and hazy talk of religious miracles were a colossal waste of time. Jefferson was therefore profoundly skeptical about many of the self-appointed roles of the established Christian churches. Setting up an elevated priestly caste was simply not to his taste. As he put in a letter of 1814, "in every country and in every age, the priest has been hostile to liberty. He is always in alliance with the despot, abetting his abuses in return for protection to his own." Priests were probably not necessary, and throughout their long history, they had abused their position of power and authority.

Crucially, however, although Jefferson was unimpressed by ritual, dogma, and priestly mischief, this did not mean that he was hostile to Christianity per se. In fact, he regarded it as a very useful basis for public morality. It was the abuse of Christianity, not its central message, to which he objected. "Of all the systems of morality," he once wrote, "none appear to me so pure as that of Jesus." His venom was reserved for all the "artificial vestments . . . [and] speculations of crazy theologians which have made a Babel of a religion the most moral and sublime ever produced by man."

Let's not forget, Jefferson was the man who spent many years poring over the New Testament searching for its edifying moral core. "I have made a wee little book," he wrote to a friend in 1813, "which I call the Philosophy of Jesus. It is a *paradigma* of his doctrines, made by cutting the text out of the book, and arranging them on the pages of a blank book, in a certain order of time or subject. A more beautiful morsel of ethics I have never seen." As Jefferson once explained, his genuine beliefs constituted something very different "from that antichristian system imputed to me by those who know nothing of my opinions." He was opposed to the "corruptions of Christianity . . . but not the genuine precepts of Jesus himself."

The 18th century produced various intellectuals who wanted to demolish the entire Christian project—the French Enlightenment was replete with such figures. Jefferson was rather different, though this hardly prevented him from being a radical. Jefferson saw absolutely nothing wrong with a painstakingly interpreted Christianity providing the bedrock for moral law. Americans being guided by the decent moral precepts explained in the Gospels was no bad thing. If they went about this work sensibly, it was a positive boon. What Christianity should never do, however, was intersect with human *positive* law—the actual rules and statutes that governed human society. On this issue Jefferson was clear: the direct entanglement of religion and politics, of what later Americans would call Church and State, was the worst idea in the world.

Jefferson devoted much of his eminent political career to hammering this message home, and the journey began in the 1770s with his attempt to promote a statute of religious freedom in Virginia. This measure would not be enacted until 1786, but even in its 1777 draft version, it neatly sums up Jefferson's aspirations and ideals. Some scholars have recently suggested that Jefferson's separationist passion was largely inspired by the attempt to attack his political enemies—that it was at least as much a matter of strategy as of principle. This seems like an unfair adjudication.

Proving himself to be a devoted follower of the philosophy of John Locke, Jefferson began his proposed statute by insisting that God had created people with free and open minds. People live their lives, and along the way, evidence and experience pour in, and opinions and beliefs are subsequently developed. The Lockeian blank slate gradually acquires its chalk marks. For a government or any source of human authority to try and coerce such minds—forcing them to believe this or that idea by means of threats or punishments—was simply wrongheaded: it was, philosophically speaking, a waste of time. Here, once again, was the very argument articulated by Williams and Penn. If the state acted in such a way, the very best that could be achieved was hypocrisy: people would pretend to believe what the state told them to believe in order to avoid censure or persecution.

At this juncture, Jefferson made a very astute remark. God, assuming that he was an omnipotent divinity, could easily have forced men to follow a specific set of opinions. Manifestly, he hadn't, and perhaps, Jefferson argued, we ought to have the good sense to follow his example. To dictate a particular interpretation of the Christian faith was flatly absurd. It was philosophically redundant, and from a practical perspective, it was disastrous: just look at all the conflicts and false religions such efforts had produced over the course of human history.

Jefferson now got specific. In Virginia, non-Anglicans were forced to pay for ministers whose beliefs they did not share, and their dissent often robbed them of civil rights and their ability to hold political office. To Jefferson, this was grotesque. You might as well say that only believers in a certain kind of geometry or physics were eligible to serve the commonwealth. It ought to be realized that "the opinions of men are not the object of civil government, nor under its jurisdiction." The magistrate should never "intrude his powers into the field of opinion."

Jefferson had his limits. If a specific religious viewpoint looked likely to provoke "overt acts against peace and good order," then the government was perfectly entitled to step in. For Jefferson, this was just common sense, and in fact, it would represent the balancing act between protecting religious freedom and preserving order and the common good that American jurisprudence would have to confront over the subsequent two centuries. In the absence of glaring threats, however, there was not the slightest reason to supervise people's beliefs or to impose orthodoxy on them. Virginia should become a place where

no man shall be compelled to frequent or support any religious worship place or ministry whatsoever, nor shall be enforced, restrained, molested or burdened in his body or goods, nor shall otherwise suffer on account of his religious opinions or belief, but that all men shall be free to profess, and by argument to maintain their opinions in matters of religion, and that the same shall in no wise diminish, enlarge, or affect their civil capacities.

After a decade's pause, Jefferson would finally triumph. His philosophy would become law.

## MADISON VERSUS HENRY

The man who did most to bring this vision to fruition—Jefferson was busy on diplomatic business in France when his proposed statute was finally enshrined in law—was another Virginian, James Madison, who had always been scandalized by religious persecution. In 1771, for instance, he roundly condemned the flogging of Baptists in Orange County, and three years later, he was appalled when the Anglicans of Culpepper parish engineered the arrest of Baptist preachers. In the same year he wrote to his good friend William Bradford in Philadelphia. The contrast between the two men's colonies could not have been more stark. In Virginia, Madison complained, the "diabolical hell-conceived principle of persecution rages among some, and to their eternal infamy the clergy can furnish their quota of imps for such business. This vexes me the most of anything whatever. There are at this time in the adjacent county not less than five or six well meaning men in close gaol for publishing their religious sentiments which in the main are very orthodox."

A few months later he explained just how envious he was of Bradford and Pennsylvania:

You are happy in dwelling in a land where those estimable privileges [of religious freedom] are fully enjoyed and [the] public has long felt the good effects of their religious as well as civil liberty. Foreigners have been encouraged to settle among you. Industry and virtue have been promoted by mutual emulation and inspection, commerce and the arts have flourished and I cannot but help attributing those continual exertions of genius which appear among you to the inspiration of liberty and that love of fame and knowledge which always accompany it. Religious bondage shackles and debilitates the mind and unfits it for every noble enterprise.

Madison was determined to put things right. In 1776 he was elected to Virginia's revolutionary convention. One of the issues confronting the assembled delegates was whether religious toleration should be enshrined in the state's constitution. George Mason came up with a draft proposal that insisted that "all men should enjoy the fullest toleration in the exercise of religion." Naturally, Madison liked this clause a great deal, but he called for an amendment that would replace the word "toleration" with "free exercise." This was a hugely important moment.

To speak of tolerance, from Madison's perspective, suggested that the state was *allowing* individuals to think and behave in certain ways, and this, in turn, implied that the state, at some unspecified time in the future, might remove this permission and make some varieties of religious expression illegal. If you referred to free exercise, however, you recognized that people enjoyed a natural right (in perpetuity) to believe and worship whatever they chose. Just as importantly you turned a negative into a positive. The word toleration always carried a judgmental charge: we don't like you, but we'll *put up with you*, for now. As Goethe famously put it, to tolerate is always to insult. The notion of genuine religious freedom, by contrast, has the potential to embrace religious difference. This book refers often to the profound difference between modern and pre-modern ways of confronting religious variety. The paradigm shift is encapsulated by this slippage from tolerance (which was always about pragmatism) to religious freedom (which was grounded in philosophical principle).

Madison got his way in 1776, and there were many victories ahead. A decade later he was the driving force behind bringing his friend Jefferson's statute for religious freedom to the Virginian statute book. The debates were hard fought in 1786. There was a broad consensus that the old model—a single religious establishment (Anglicanism) being paid for through everyone's taxes, regardless of their personal beliefs—should be abandoned. Some politicians (with Patrick Henry leading the charge) wanted only to tinker with the status quo, however.

Henry had long been convinced that "a general toleration of religion appears . . . the best means of peopling our country." He once argued that "the free exercise of religion has stocked the northern part of the continent with inhabitants," but that owing to unprogressive legislation, "a Calvinist, a Lutheran, or Quaker sails not to Virginia." Under his general assessment scheme, the notion of a single established church supported by every citizen's tax dollars would be abandoned. Instead, the state would continue to levy taxes to support religion, but each individual taxpayer could nominate which church was to receive the taxes he paid. As Henry's proposed bill explained,

Whereas the general diffusion of Christian knowledge hath a natural tendency to correct the morals of men, restrain their vices, and preserve the peace of society; which cannot be effected without a competent provision for learned teachers, who may be thereby enabled to devote their time and attention to the duty of instructing such citizens, as from their circumstances and want of education, cannot otherwise attain such knowledge; and it is judged that such provision may be made by the Legislature, without counteracting the liberal principle heretofore adopted and intended to be preserved by abolishing all distinctions of pre-eminence amongst the different societies or communities of Christians.

Be it therefore enacted by the General Assembly, That for the support of Christian teachers, per centum on the amount, or in the pound on the sum payable for tax on the property within this Commonwealth, is hereby assessed, and shall be paid by every person chargeable with the said tax at the time the same shall become due; and the Sheriffs of the several Counties shall have power to levy and collect the same in the same manner and under the like restrictions and limitations, as are or may be prescribed by the laws for raising the Revenues of this State.

And be it enacted, That for every sum so paid, the Sheriff or Collector shall give a receipt, expressing therein to what society of Christians the person from whom he may receive the same shall direct the money to be paid, keeping a distinct account thereof in his books.

This was envisaged as a way for the state to support religion in an evenhanded, non-exclusive manner; outlawing a single state religion was one thing, but outlawing all state support for religion was quite another. As Henry insisted, a successful government simply could not survive without the help of Christian institutions: they were the surest guarantor of decent private and public morality, and to rely on voluntary contributions would be disastrous for all of the state's religious groups.

For Madison, this did not go nearly far enough. It still involved the entanglement of Church and State. In his *Memorial and Remonstrance,* Madison pleaded with his contemporaries to embrace the idea that religious belief should be "wholly exempt" from the cognizance of civil society. A state demanding taxes to support churches, even in a more equitable way, was still a state demanding taxes. This brought the threat of force into the business of religious belief. States, because they were built on the idea of potential coercion, couldn't help but do this, and this posed a potential challenge to a person's "unalienable right" to let his conscience guide his religious beliefs.

Into the bargain, taking the state completely out of the question might just turn out to be excellent news for Christianity. We should remember, Madison suggested, that before the days of Constantine, "this religion both existed and flourished, not only without the support of human laws, but in spite of every opposition from them." The Church did not require the crutch of state support, and as history showed, when such support had arrived, the results had been parlous: centuries' worth of persecution.

It was time for America to remember the best parts of its colonial history, when it had provided "an asylum to the persecuted and oppressed of every nation and religion." This, Madison sang, was a "lustre to our country." The rival legal model Madison was trying to defeat—multiple establishment—was a step backward: "from the Inquisition it differs . . . only in degree." If it was enacted, it would deter the seeker after religious freedom from settling in Virginia. It would be "a beacon on our coast, warning him to seek some other haven."

Madison (with lots of help, notably from Baptists such as John Leland) won the day. For Madison, looking back in later life, his greatest success, his proudest achievement in the work of creating religious freedom, lay in Virginia. "Some of the states," he lamented, "have not embraced this just and this truly Christian principle in its proper latitude," but "there is one state at least, Virginia, where religious liberty is placed on its true foundation."

## CONSTITUTION AND AMENDMENT

In fact, so far as history is concerned, Madison would achieve even greater triumphs, most memorably his role in defining the federal government's attitude toward religious freedom and State–Church relations: as the First Amendment confidently put it, "Congress shall make no law respecting an establishment of religion, or prohibiting the free exercise thereof."

The road to this final phraseology was rocky. Dozens of proposed amendments had battled for supremacy. One of Madison's initial drafts, for instance, read, "The civil rights of none shall be abridged on account of religious belief or worship, nor shall any national religion be established, nor shall the full and equal rights of conscience be in any manner, or under any pretext infringed." In committee, this was quite reasonably seen as rather cumbersome. Eventually the clause "No religion shall be established by law, nor shall the equal rights of conscience be infringed" was proposed. Madison then suggested returning the word "national" to the clause—a sure indicator that, even at this early stage, there was much debate about whether the proposed amendment was intended to apply simply to the federal government or to the various states of the Union as well. Finally, it was decided to refer to limitations being applied to the actions of "Congress", and after yet more manipulation and revision, the amendment with which we are all now familiar entered the statute book.

In consort with article 6 of the Constitution—"no religious test shall ever be required as a qualification to any office or public trust under the United States"—America now seemed to have decided its approach to Church–State relations. In fact, though, the struggle to interpret such words was far from over. It continues to this day.

***

To some Americans there was a sense of unfinished business from the outset. If Isaac Backus was famous, his fellow Baptist John Leland took on almost legendary status. Leland had made a decisive contribution to the Virginian campaign to establish religious freedom in 1786, and a persistent rumor tells how James Madison visited Leland after returning from the Constitutional Convention to calm Baptist fears about the lack of protection of religious liberty in the Constitution. Whether or not such a meeting took place, Leland's support was crucial in securing Madison the position as Orange County's delegate to the Virginia ratifying convention. When Madison was elected to Congress in 1789, Leland once more intervened and was sure to stress the need for further constitutional guarantees of religious liberty. His was one of the voices that helped convert Madison to the need for a Bill of Rights, a measure that today strikes us an inevitability but that at the time was a hotly contested issue.

Leland was presumably delighted with the arrival of the First Amendment, but he still had goals to achieve. He moved north in 1791, returning to his native Massachusetts—a place in which ideas of establishment and

Congregational dominance were still deeply entrenched. Leland spent much of the next decades seeking, in print and pulpit, to overturn the ecclesiastical status quo in both Massachusetts and Connecticut, perhaps most energetically in his writings in *The Yankee Spy, Calculated for the Religious Meridian of Massachusetts.*

He repeatedly confronted the question of Church–State separation head-on, arguing against the payment of chaplains from public funds and for the right of the U.S. Post Office to remain open on Sundays. Crucially, Leland rooted his advocacy of religious liberty not only in a philosophical allegiance to John Locke but also in an awareness of history. He recounted, in great detail, the troubled story of the Baptist faith during Virginia's colonial period: "Soon after the Baptist ministers began to preach in Virginia," he recalled at the start of the 1790s, "the novelty of their doctrine, the rarity of mechanics and planters preaching such strange things; and the wonderful effect that their preaching had on the people, called out multitudes to hear them." But such popularity "made them many enemies." Inevitably, the "usual alarm of the church and state being in danger, was echoed through the colony." The clerics and supporters of the established churches began to cry, "like the silver-smith of old . . . 'our craft is in danger of being set at naught.'" Decades of prejudice and persecution were the unhappy result.

It came as no surprise, then, that he believed "that civil rulers have nothing to do with religion, in their official capacities." This, he opined, was "interwoven in the Baptist plan." A principle was at stake. "The legitimate powers of government," Leland insisted, "extend only to punish men for working ill to their neighbors, and no ways effect the rights of conscience." With an eye to history, Leland argued that it did not matter that "the nation of Israel received their civil and religious laws from Jehovah, which were binding on them, and no other." With the "extirpation of that nation," such a compact was abolished. This was old news. For the United States of America, a modern Christian commonwealth, to establish itself on "the same claim" would be presumptuous. So far as Leland was aware, it had not received "the same charter from heaven." What was legitimate in the age of Moses was not necessarily legitimate in the 1790s.

From Leland's perspective, religious establishments turned people into either fools or hypocrites; they bred violence and banished virtue. Only error needed the help of government to support it. In its "purest ages," religion "made its way in the world, not only without the aid of law, but against all the laws of haughty monarchs, and all the maxims of the schools." So long as abuse was outlawed, "government should protect every man in thinking and speaking freely." Echoing Madison, and moving a novel concept forward, Leland revealed, the "liberty I contend for, is more than toleration. The very idea of toleration is despicable, it supposes that some have a pre-eminence above the rest, to grant indulgence; whereas all should be equally free, Jews, Turks, Pagans and Christians." There should be no test oaths, no general tax assessments in support of religion: such an assessment made preachers into ministers of state; it turned "the gospel into merchandise, and sinks religion upon a level with other things."

It was not even legitimate for civil government "to establish fixed holy days for divine worship." Leland was "not an enemy to holy days"; he merely believed that appointing them was "no part of human legislation." Nor should civil and military chaplains be paid "out of the public treasury." "If legislatures choose to have a chaplain, for heaven's sake let them pay him by contributions, and not out of the public chest." Likewise, for "chaplains to go into the army, is about as good economy as it was for Israel to carry the ark of God to battle . . . instead of reclaiming the people, they generally are corrupted themselves, as the ark fell into the hands of the Philistines." The crucial point was that ministers might start to say something along the lines of "if you will pay me well for preaching and praying, I will do them, otherwise I will not." Such "golden sermons and silver prayers," Leland suggested, "are of no great value."

What should we make of John Leland? There was clearly something epochal about a profoundly religious man arguing for an American separation of Church and State as complete as any that had come before. Leland took things to a more radical extreme than Isaac Backus, and in the wake of the First Amendment, he worked inordinately hard, with limited success, to extend his vision to the state politics of New England. He represents the acceptance of a need for rigorous separatism (proof positive that such ideas were in the air during the 1790s), and there is something astonishing in the fact that his meditations touched on so many issues that would puzzle and divide Americans for the next two centuries.

In fact, if everyone had shared Leland's (or Madison's) opinions, everything would have been set fair, and interpreting and applying the First Amendment would have been wonderfully straightforward. As things turned out, the Leland agenda was not the only game in town. Carrying forward America's new approach to Church–State affairs would prove to be more difficult than anyone could have imagined in those balmy post-revolutionary days.

## SUGGESTED READING

The literature on both Jefferson and Madison is vast. Good starting points are, for Jefferson, Daniel Dreisbach, *Thomas Jefferson and the Wall of Separation between Church and State* (New York, 2002); J. J. Ellis, *American Sphinx: The Character of*

*Thomas Jefferson* (New York, 1997); Edwin S. Gaustad, *Sworn on the Altar of God: A Religious Biography of Thomas Jefferson* (Grand Rapids, MI, 1996); Charles B. Sanford, *The Religious Life of Thomas Jefferson* (Charlottesville, VA, 1984); Garret Ward Sheldon and Daniel Dreisbach, eds., *Religion and Political Culture in Jefferson's Virginia* (Lanham, MD, 2000).

And for Madison, see Robert S. Alley, ed., *James Madison and Religious Liberty* (Buffalo, NY, 1985); Lance Banning, "James Madison, the Statute for Religious Freedom and the Crisis of Republican Convictions," in *The Virginia Statute for Religious Freedom: Its Evolution and Consequences in American History*, ed. Merrill D. Peterson and Robert C Vaughan (New York, 1988); Lance Banning, *The Sacred Fire of Liberty: James Madison and the Founding of the Federal Republic* (Ithaca, NY, 1995); C. Emmerich, "The Enigma of James Madison on Church and State," in *Religion, Public Life and the American Polity*, ed. Luis Lugo (Knoxville, TN, 1994), 51–73; Jack N. Rakove, *James Madison and the Creation of the American Republic* (Glenview, IL, 1990).

On Virginia in general, see Thomas E. Buckley, *Church and State in Revolutionary Virginia, 1776–1787* (Charlottesville, VA, 1977).

On the genesis of the First Amendment, see Thomas J. Curry, *The First Freedoms. Church and State in America to the Passage of the First Amendment* (New York, 1986), and for broader analysis of the intentions of the founding fathers and the late 18th-century philosophical climate, see Chris Beneke, *Beyond Toleration: The Religious Origins of American Pluralism* (New York, 2006); Philip Hamburger, *Separation of Church and State* (Cambridge, MA, 2002); Charles P. Hanson, *Necessary Virtue: The Pragmatic Origins of Religious Liberty in New England* (Charlottesville, VA, 1998); James Hutson, *Religion and the Founding of the American Republic* (Washington, D.C: 1998); James Hutson, *Forgotten Features of the Founding: The Recovery of Religious Themes in the Early American Republic* (Lanham, MD, 2003); Frank Lambert, *The Founding Fathers and the Place of Religion in America* (Princeton, NJ, 2003).

# 5

# Consequences: The 19th Century

Present-day debates about Church and State are, quite rightly, often concerned with the intentions of the United States' founding fathers and the legislative documents they produced. We have just seen some of the tussles between Jefferson, Madison, and their rivals, and when considering the conclusions that were reached, there is more than antiquarian interest at stake. We are obliged to ask how people living in the 21st century should set about utilizing and interpreting those conclusions. Bluntly put, how much do past thoughts and actions matter when confronting today's Church–State issues?

## INTERPRETATIONS

Some would argue for a rigorist interpretation of the nation's founding documents: taking the words of the First Amendment, for example, in their most obvious sense and avoiding unnecessarily inventive or flexible interpretations. In this scheme of things, the original pronouncements on religious freedom and Church–State relations can be seen as fixed, even adamantine.

This approach has clear benefits: it appears to demonstrate fidelity to the founders' vision, and at least in theory, it ought to produce a coherent and consistent way of proceeding. From a purely legal perspective, it is the most straightforward option available: the letter of the law is the letter of the law. There are also drawbacks to this strategy, however. First, it assumes that an obvious interpretation of the 14 words of the First Amendment is easily available, but as the evidence shows (and as we are about to see), this patently isn't the case. Second, an overly rigorist approach is apt to diminish the importance of historical change and development. Even if we could demonstrate that the First Amendment is amenable to an uncontested interpretation, does this mean that its ideals and aspirations ought to be applied, directly and without alteration or manipulation, to the America of the 21st century?

With this question in mind, some legal and constitutional experts have preferred to adopt a more organic approach. The Constitution and the First Amendment, they aver, are to be revered, but when applying their commandments, we should be cognizant of the fact that times and political circumstances are apt to change. In his concurring opinion in the Supreme Court case of *Abington v. Schempp* in 1963 (a case we discuss in the next chapter), Justice William Brennan suggested that "the line which separates the secular from the sectarian in American life is elusive." It was always difficult to define that boundary because of a paradox that was "central to our scheme of liberty." "While our institutions reflect a firm conviction that we are a religious people, those institutions by solemn constitutional injunction may not officially involve religion in such a way as to prefer, discriminate against, or oppress, a particular sect or religion."

Brennan conceded that interpreting this injunction was always destined to be complicated, and "an awareness of history and an appreciation of the aims of the founding fathers do not always resolve concrete problems." In the specific matter under discussion in *Abington v. Schempp,* religion in modern public schools, it was impossible to know exactly what Jefferson or Madison would have thought. America was simply not the same place now that it had been during the 1790s. For one thing, "our religious composition makes us a vastly more diverse people than were our forefathers. They knew differences chiefly among Protestant sects. Today the nation is far more heterogeneous religiously, including as it does substantial minorities not only of Catholics and Jews but as well of those who worship according to no version of the Bible and those who worship no God at all."

Brennan argued that "a too literal quest for the advice of the founding fathers upon the issues of these cases seems to me futile and misdirected." Most importantly, "the historical record is at best ambiguous, and statements can readily be found to support either side of the proposition." It was always wise to be aware of the "ambiguity of history." Ultimately, Brennan doubted whether "their view, even if perfectly clear one way or the other, would supply a dispositive answer to the question presented by these cases."

Of course, this didn't mean that present-day generations were entirely adrift from tradition. Far from it. The skill was not to look for specific advice but to strive to translate "the majestic generalities of the Bill of Rights, conceived as part of the pattern of liberal government in the eighteenth century, into concrete restraints on officials dealing with the problems of the twentieth century."

This remains sound advice, but when trying to capture those majestic generalities—to capture their spirit—there is much room to argue about what those founding documents actually said and intended. On first inspection, the religion clauses of the First Amendment can look very straightforward. Dig a little deeper, and all manner of puzzling issues begin to emerge. Even capturing a general sense of what they intended—which almost everyone would agree is a worthwhile pursuit—is fraught with difficulties.

First, how representative of contemporary opinion were the ideas enshrined in the First Amendment? It is easy to assume that the pronouncements of the United States' founding documents represented a consensus of late 18th-century opinion. This would certainly give them additional legal clout, but it is perhaps a questionable proposition. As we've seen, Jefferson and Madison won in Virginia and via the First Amendment, at federal level, but it could certainly be argued that their position on Church and State was far from being normative. Men such as Madison and Jefferson (who played a starring role in defining and legislating the new republic's political identity) shared a belief in a broad religious freedom, and their writings seem to indicate a commitment to a relatively rigorous separation between sacred and secular matters—at least at the level of direct entanglement. As we've also seen, however, many of their contemporaries were possessed of less radical philosophical sympathies. Patrick Henry, for instance, was no maverick: he enjoyed broad support.

This is obviously a very awkward proposition; it raises the possibility that some of the foundational legal principles enshrined in state and federal constitutions and amendments did not articulate contemporary majority opinion: not exactly the ideal beginning for a new republic that prided itself on reflecting and protecting the will of the people. There is also the tricky issue that the various state constitutions of the early Republic disagreed violently about how to proceed in the business of Church-State encounters. The very notion of a coherent "founding fathers' vision" therefore begins to look a lot like a chimera.

Second, and here we return to more concrete issues, there is also the surprisingly contested question of what the First Amendment actually implies. It would be reasonable to argue that the amendment sought to outlaw the federal government from sponsoring a single national religion. What the amendment does not make clear is whether this Church–State separation was also meant to be operative at the state level: the amendment talks about what *Congress* should and should not do. It says nothing about the expected behavior of local legislatures. Crucially, the individual states had, in theory, a much broader legislative remit. They had general powers (an ability to act according to whatever rubrics their specific constitutions decided), whereas Congress's powers were, from the outset, circumscribed.

This has provoked endless squabbles (which continue to this day) about how the clauses of the First Amendment ought to be applied to the various states of the Union. What is supposed to happen when a particular state's take on Church–State relations seems to contradict the rules under which the federal government is expected to operate? This hermeneutic gap was theoretically plugged by the Fourteenth Amendment, which, in essence, insisted that the rights everyone enjoyed as a citizen of the United States couldn't be assaulted by the idiosyncratic laws and statutes of a particular state. In theory, this should have stymied unnecessary quarrels between local and federal government. Self-evidently, it didn't, and in the sphere of Church–State relations, this is largely because of the inherent ambiguity of the First Amendment's religion clauses. Was the amendment supposed to apply to the states, or was it a strictly federal injunction? It is clear that those such as Madison wanted its prohibitions to enjoy the widest possible currency, but as the history of early 19th-century America amply demonstrates, there were many people who did not share his agenda.

I have mentioned ambiguity, and in this arena, the First Amendment had other tricks up its sleeve. It could be argued that the amendment sought only to prevent direct entanglement of Church and State—tax dollars funding specific denominations, elected political leaders becoming directly involved in religious tussles, and so forth. The unanswered question is whether this was meant to signal an absolute schism between faith and politics. The answer seems to be no.

For better or worse, during the 19th century the vast majority of Americans remained committed to the idea that Christianity (by which they usually meant *Protestant* Christianity) should play a major role in defining and guiding the new nation's morality. There was to be religious freedom (though, as we'll see, even this was decidedly attenuated), and the national government was not to sponsor the agenda of a specific denomination, but this didn't mean that the fundamental moral nostrums of Christianity suddenly became irrelevant. Even some of the most vigorous champions of religious freedom—Isaac Backus and Thomas Jefferson included—would presumably have had some sympathy with this analysis.

In other words, distinguishing between Church and State was not the same thing as separating religion and politics. Legislation was one thing; the contours of American public and intellectual life were quite another. As many historians have averred, 19th-century America was still very much a de facto

Christian nation. This delighted some and infuriated others—not least those of non-Protestant beliefs, members of non-Christian religions, and a growing constituency who chose to believe in no God at all.

Bold and efficient as they were, the words of the First Amendment did not put an end to controversy. Whether this interpretative morass should have any impact on present-day public policy is far from clear. Just because 19th-century Americans held the moral import of Christianity in high esteem does not necessarily imply that it should enjoy the same privileged position today. As ever, though, we are obliged to treat the 19th century on its own terms. It is fair to say that the people of that century had an awfully hard time deciding what the First Amendment meant for the future of Christianity in America. The controversial issue of Church–State relations was not easy to resolve.

\*\*\*

Let's turn to the first of the conundrums mentioned previously: the degree to which the First Amendment was supposed to apply to individual states. In the case of *Barron v. Baltimore* in 1833, Chief Justice John Marshall argued that the Bill of Rights should not be recklessly abused in order to limit state powers. Technically, the roster of amendments placed limits on the actions of only the federal government: "They contained no expression indicating an intention to apply them to the state governments. This court cannot so apply them." This position was effectively overturned (or at least much threatened) by the arrival of the Fourteenth Amendment in 1866. As the amendment pronounced, "no state shall make or enforce any law which shall abridge the privileges or immunities of the citizens of the United States, nor shall any state deprive any person of life, liberty or property without due process of law; nor deny to any person within its jurisdiction the equal protection of the laws."

The most straightforward translation of this legalese is that although individual states were perfectly entitled to enact their own laws, such laws became offensive when they assaulted the protections that every American citizen enjoyed under the terms of the federal constitution and its subsequent amendments.

This was a very astute, and very necessary, piece of legislation, but unsurprisingly, it has been rather difficult to enforce. The various states of the Union are very protective of their legislative independence: it might even be said that there has always been a strong undercurrent in American history that resents the national government intruding on the affairs of individual states. The Hollywood cliché, whereby local law-enforcement agencies are aggravated by the arrival of sharp-suited members of the FBI, has become a cliché for good reason.

When dealing with the consequences of the Fourteenth Amendment that, in theory, could impact a huge range of local political decisions, America has tended to abide by the principle of "selective incorporation." In other words, it has seemed prudent to limit the application of the amendment to very specific circumstances: usually, when the attack on a right or a protection has been seen as especially flagrant. It might be suggested that this is something of a fudge. Strictly speaking, that is probably an accurate assessment, but in order to prevent federal courtrooms from being overrun by cases (most of which would have been flimsy), it was probably a sensible approach.

There is no better example of this tendency than the issues of religious freedom and Church–State relations. It would take almost a century for the clauses of the Fourteenth Amendment to be applied directly to Supreme Court cases that dealt with these subjects. Even today, the issue of what a state such as Arkansas or Texas ought to be able to do in the arena of Church–State relations within its own borders is still very sensitive. With predictable frequency, state legislatures enact laws that seem to contradict the clauses of the First Amendment.

Back in the early days of the Republic, long before the Fourteenth Amendment came into being, this battle between national and state law was even more hard fought. Some states fell immediately into line with the aspirations of the First Amendment and the oath-banning clause of the Constitution. Others did not. Officials in Pennsylvania still had to take an oath that declared their belief in God, thus ruling out atheists from public duty. In Maryland, taxes continued to be raised to support ministers, and in Massachusetts the idea of multiple establishment secured legislative approval in 1780.

As the state's founding documents variously explained, "the happiness of a people, and the good order and preservation of civil government, essentially depend on piety, religion and morality." It was therefore "the right as well as the duty of all men in society, publicly, and at stated seasons, to worship the Supreme Being, the great creator and preserver of the universe." The notion that a single denomination should dominate state support was abandoned. From now on, a taxpayer would be allowed to earmark his contributions to support whichever church he chose: a Congregationalist could fund Congregationalism, a Baptist could help pay the wages of a Baptist minister, and so on, but he still had to pay taxes in support of *someone*. This, in a nutshell, was Patrick Henry's vision of multiple establishment come to life.

The state was perfectly entitled "to authorize and require the several towns, parishes, precincts, and other bodies politic . . . to make suitable provision, at their own expense, for the institution of the public worship of God, and for the support and maintenance of public Protestant teachers of piety, religion and morality."

Massachusetts was not alone, and whatever the First Amendment said, some version of religious establishment remained operative in Vermont until 1807, in New Hampshire until 1817, in Connecticut until 1818, and in Massachusetts itself until 1833.

It is worth pointing out that the battles to overturn these religious settlements were extremely ill-humored: a sure indication that there was little concord on the issue of Church–State relations in the early Republic. They dominated the politics of various states during the first decades of the 19th century. In Connecticut, for example, a law of 1801 reinforced the idea of a dominant Congregational Church. Members of minority faiths—whether Episcopalians, Methodists, or Baptists—were still obliged to provide the state with formal declarations of their dissent in order to avoid general taxation.

John Leland, for all his earlier victories, was still obliged to fight battles during the early 19th century, attacking the "the mischief of Connecticut religion." Eventually, a Republican-Episcopalian group, under the leadership of Oliver Wolcott Jr., rose up against Congregational dominance and called for a state constitutional convention aimed at securing total disestablishment. Such moves offended supporters of the status quo.

Jasper Adams, the president of Charleston College, was especially unhappy: "that Christianity has no connexion with our civil constitutions of government" was one of the "absurd and dangerous consequences" of disestablishment. It would lead to the destruction of "Christian morals, Christian sentiments and Christian principles," and it represented an "attitude of open and uncompromising hostility to every form and every degree of the Christian faith." This was polemic at its best (or worst), but it represented a far from uncommon attitude.

Some equally conservative religious leaders did begin to discern some benefit in drawing sharper lines between Church and State. When Connecticut finally decided to embrace disestablishment, the minister Lyman Beecher was devastated. He was convinced that it would provoke political factionalism and moral breakdown and rob the community's natural moral leaders of their just authority. Beecher was convinced that "the injury done to the cause of Christ, as we then supposed, was irrevocable. For several days I suffered what no tongue can tell." Gradually, however, Beecher came to the conclusion that, in fact, it was "the best thing that ever happened to the state of Connecticut. It cut the churches loose from dependence on state support. It threw them wholly on their own resources and on God." Competing denominations would have to fight their own corner, without state support, and so, Beecher calculated, the cream would rise to the top.

Others were not so sanguine, and when Massachusetts went through a similar process of disestablishment in the early 1830s, old arguments were rehashed and familiar battle lines were drawn. The question of whether individual states were obliged to follow the lead of the federally intended First Amendment showed few signs of disappearing. It can safely be suggested that such questions are still very much with us.

## DE FACTO DOMINANCE?

During the United States' first few decades, there were clear signs that some Americans did not want Christianity to lose its grip on public morality or to be banished entirely from the political decision-making process. Some even thought it was regrettable that there was no mention of God in the nation's Constitution, such as the irked minister who complained to George Washington that there was no "explicit acknowledgement of the only true God and Jesus Christ who he sent . . . somewhere in the Magna Carta of our country."

Washington's own religious opinions have long been the subject of frenzied debate, but in his farewell address of September 1796, he at least suggested that religion was the "necessary spring of popular government." For John Adams, meanwhile, religion established "the principles upon which freedom and security stand." A "decent respect for Christianity," and he meant Protestant Christianity, was "among the best recommendations for the public service."

There were even moments of rather obvious entanglement between religion and the federal government during these decades. Admittedly, some early political documents from the early Republic do seem to hint at the possibility that America was not being conceptualized as a Christian nation. The famous article 11 of the 1797 Treaty of Tripoli, signed to smooth relations with the nations of North Africa, had this to say:

As the Government of the United States of America is not, in any sense, founded on the Christian religion; as it has in itself no character of enmity against the laws, religion, or tranquillity, of Mussulmen; and, as the said States never entered into any war, or act of hostility against any Mahometan nation, it is declared by the parties, that no pretext arising from religious opinions, shall ever produce an interruption of the harmony existing between the two countries.

Other documents and trends seem to tell a rather different story, however. The North West Ordinance, designed for the governance of lands beyond the Ohio, declared in 1787 that because "religion, morality and knowledge" were "necessary to good government and the happiness of mankind," religiously minded "schools and the means of education shall forever be encouraged."

When a cholera epidemic struck the nation in 1832, the Senate proposed a resolution calling for the president to declare a national day of prayer and fasting. Both Andrew Jackson and the House rejected the measure, precisely because it was seen as breaching the divide between Church and State, but such a day of prayer was endorsed in 12 separate states, and even more significantly, when a similar notion was proposed during epidemics in 1848–1849, it was supported by President Zachary Taylor.

Of course, many Americans argued for a more separationist approach, and throughout these years, moments of direct entanglement between Church and State were far, far less common than during the colonial era. All told, however, a majority of people in the early Republic seem to have been broadly committed to the idea that although the days of state-supported churches were coming to an end, Christianity should still serve as a moral compass.

When the Frenchman Alexis de Tocqueville visited the nation during the 1830s, he recognized that thanks to the First Amendment, religion played "no direct part in the government of society," but it was still to "be regarded as the first of their political institutions." There was "no country in the world where the Christian religion retains a greater hold over the souls of men than in America."

America, by many accounts, was still a Christian nation, and perhaps paradoxically, this was precisely because of the rubrics of the First Amendment. Churches of all complexions were able to prosper and were obliged to fall back on their own energies and resources. Many, Tocqueville concluded, "attributed the peaceful dominion of religion in their country to the separation of church and state."

One minister, Robert Baird, summed up a not uncommon attitude. He fully accepted the legal separation of Church and State, and he reveled in the benefits of voluntarism, but he still insisted that religious faith had much to offer political life: "It receives the immense moral influence of the church—of the preaching of the gospel, at so many thousand and tens of thousand of points, all over the land—of the Sabbath school—of the Bible class, and all the other influences of Christianity. It is in these that the laws find their surest basis, and their most effective sanction." It was because of the continuing influence of Christianity "that a vast country of more than twenty seven millions of people can be governed, and is governed, without the bayonet and the cannon."

*\*\**

The first decades of the 19th century can be seen as an attempt to tease out the consequences of the First Amendment and American's newfound commitment to Church–State separation. Take one of the era's most influential jurists, Joseph Story, for instance. Like many of his contemporaries, Story was convinced that Christianity still had a vital role to play in American public life. He believed that Thomas Jefferson, for example, had gone much too far in his efforts to dampen down Christianity's influence. Having read a collection of Jefferson's works in 1830, Story described them to a friend in decidedly negative terms: "Have you seen Mr Jefferson's *Works*?" "If not, sit down at once and read his fourth volume. It is the most pernicious melange of all sorts of scandals you ever read. It will elevate your opinion of his talents, but lower him in point of principle and morals not a little."

Story's particular bone of contention was that Jefferson had consistently argued that Christianity was not a part of English Common Law, and therefore, by extension, it had no obvious place in the laws of the Republic, which in many ways were rooted in the English Common Law tradition. Story's researches provoked a rather different conclusion. He pointed to the ancient tradition of English courts protecting Christianity, punishing heresy and blasphemy.

Story was so passionate on this issue because of his broader commitment to sustaining the role of Christianity in the Republic. He thought of Christianity as the bedrock of social stability and order, and he had a particular vision of how it should pervade American culture. Church and State, he opined, shared a common goal: the encouragement of public and private virtue. Clerics would preach their sermons, and the state would enforce laws and provide the material conditions in which good Christian morality might flourish. Story was certainly not a supporter of theocracy, and he often wrote about the perils of eroding the establishment clause of the First Amendment. What he could not stomach was the idea that Church and State, given their shared objectives, should enjoy no sort of relationship whatsoever.

In his 1833 commentaries on the Constitution, Story elaborated at great length on this theme. He turned to the constitutional prohibition of religious oaths for public officials, and in many ways, he proved himself to be a textbook separationist. This was "not introduced merely for the purpose of satisfying the scruples of many respectable persons who feel an invincible repugnance to any religious test . . . It had a higher object: to cut off forever every pretence of any alliance between church and state in the national government." The framers saw such dangers "marked out in the history of other ages and countries."

One need only look at the history of the Reformation, he suggested, and the persecutors and martyrs it produced. England itself had seen its share of state-sponsored bigotry, and those who sought to prove that anti-dissenting legislation had at least not been enforced as harshly as it might have been were resorting to a feeble argument: "the meanest apologist of the worst enormities of a Roman Emperor could not have shadowed out a defence more servile." America had thus made a wise decision: it was easy "to foresee that without some prohibition of religious tests, a successful sect in our country might, by once possessing power, pass test laws which would secure to themselves a monopoly of all the offices of trust and profit under the national government."

So far, this was as separationist as anything Jefferson might have said. Nonetheless, Story remained insistent that one could not simply shut Christianity out of public life and discourse. Turning to the religion clauses of the First Amendment, he suggested that few would contest that "piety, religion and morality are intimately connected with the well-being of the state, and indispensable to the administration of civil justice." Any society needed its references to God, providence, and the rewards and punishments of heaven and hell. It was "difficult to conceive how any civilised society can well exist without them," and it was "impossible for those who believe in the truth of Christianity as a divine revelation to doubt that it is the especial duty of government to foster and encourage it among all the citizens and subjects."

The trickier dilemma lay in deciding what limits ought to be placed on this fostering and encouraging. There were, Story explained, several options. There could be an ecclesiastical establishment of a single religion that still left people free to worship wherever and however they saw fit. Or there might be such an establishment that "excludes all persons not belonging to it, either wholly or in part, from any participation in the public honours, trusts, emoluments, privileges and immunities of the state."

The United States had made its choice, and the idea of the *federal* government erecting a *national* church had rightly been cast out. The founders had not sought to encourage Islam or Judaism, but to "exclude all rivalry among Christian sects and to prevent any national ecclesiastical establishment." America had learned the dangers of certain kinds of religious settlement. After all, those persecuted Puritans who had fled to New England "would furnish out a chapter as full of the darkest bigotry and intolerance as any which could be found to disgrace the pages of foreign annals."

With so many sects, it was "impossible that there should not arise perpetual strife and perpetual jealousy on the subject of ecclesiastical ascendancy if the national government were left free to create a religious establishment. The only security was in extirpating the power . . . thus the whole power over the subject of religion is left exclusively to the state governments." But this did not alter the fact that there were "few persons in this or any other Christian country who would deliberately contend that it was unreasonable or unjust to foster and encourage the Christian religion generally." It remained undeniable that, as the Massachusetts Bill of Rights explained, "the happiness of a people and the good order and preservation of civil government essentially depend upon piety, religion and morality."

The solution, therefore, was to accept—and this had been just as true at the time of the constitutional settlement—that the "general if not the universal sentiment in America was that Christianity ought to receive encouragement from the state so far as was not in competition with private rights of conscience and the freedom of religious worship." There had been no ambition to level all religions or encourage indifferentism.

When Story referred to Christianity, he usually meant Protestant Christianity, and he believed that the United States was involved in a test case where it would be proven that no free government was likely to survive without the influence of Christian morality. Assuredly, the state did not possess a right to force the consciences of other men, to punish them for their religious behavior. After all, as had been argued from everyone from John Locke onward, religious faith could never be instilled through coercion. Story remained confident that, even within a society permeated by Christian mores and morals, "the Catholic and the Protestant, the Calvinist and the Armenian, the Jew and the infidel" would be able to "sit down at the common table of the national councils without any inquisition into their faith or mode of worship." For all that, such permeation was still vital. "The future experience of Christendom and chiefly of the American states must settle this problem." Christianity should be generally encouraged by government.

Story was not alone in his analysis of America culture. We have already seen the Rev. Jasper Adams, president of the College of Charleston, fuming at disestablishment in Connecticut. When he published a printed version of his sermon on the *Relation of Christianity to Civil Government in the United States,* he sent Story a copy. Adams's fundamental point was that "the people of the United States have retained the Christian religion as the foundation of their civil, legal and political institutions." Story revealed that he had "read it with uncommon satisfaction." "My own private judgement," he wrote, "has long been (and every day's experience more and more confirms me in it) that government cannot long exist without an alliance with religion to some extent and that Christianity is indispensable to the true interests and solid foundations of all free governments." Story voiced real concerns about the indifference with which the American people "seem in our day to be disposed to cut adrift from old principles."

Another ally of Story's was James Kent. Kent regarded Story's constitutional commentaries as a "bold and free defence of sound doctrine against the insidious, mischievous and malignant attacks of Jefferson . . . an incomparable monument of sound and healthy constitutional principles." In 1811, in his capacity as chief justice of New York's highest court, Kent confidently declared that "we are a Christian people and the morality of this country is deeply engrained upon Christianity and not upon the doctrines of worship of impostors."

Kent put his gavel where his mouth was. In the case of *People v. Ruggles,* the accused was indicted for profaning Christ and the Virgin Mary. There was no specific New York law against blasphemy, but from Kent's perspective, this simply didn't matter. The crime of blasphemy had long been denounced in the English Common Law Tradition (remember the tussle between Jefferson and Story), and this was good enough for Kent. Ruggles had "wickedly, maliciously, and blasphemously uttered in the presence and hearing of diverse good and Christian people these false, feigned, scandalous . . . words, to wit: 'Jesus Christ was a bastard and his mother must be a whore.'"

Such statements were always likely to cause offense, Kent suggested, because "the people of this state, in common with the people of this country, profess the eternal doctrines of Christianity, as the rule of their faith and practice; and to scandalize the author of these doctrines is not only, in a religious point of view, extremely impious, but even in respect to the obligations due to society, is a gross violation of decency and good order."

***

I have dwelled on the ideas of men such as Story and Kent not because they were the only fashionable ideas in the early Republic, but because they are often overlooked. Of course, many Americans agreed wholeheartedly with the conclusions of Jefferson and Madison, but it is worth remembering that such conclusions remained deeply controversial. The question of what the constitutional prohibitions of Church–State entanglement meant for the future of American Christianity was deeply controversial.

It is also fair to say that, in the posturing of someone such as James Kent, a partisan, exclusively Protestant outlook was probably taken to excess. Gross generalizations about what the "American people" believed were already, even in the 1810s, quickly becoming obsolete. Arguing about the application of the law was a fairly innocuous activity. More troubling was the question of how this idea of America still being a Protestant Christian nation would impact upon the ever-expanding non-Protestant population—not to mention those people whose Protestantism sat outside the mainstream.

The point here is that the relationship between faith and politics was always about more than the measures outlined in the statute book. If there *was* a general sense that the nation's politics and morality ought to be guided by the precepts of mainstream Protestant Christianity, what would this mean for those of more radical Protestant or non-Protestant sympathies? Here we enter a very confusing, sometime unedifying period in America's religious history.

*** 

It is easy (because it is accurate) to claim that Protestantism was the dominant religious force in 19th-century America. There were many varieties of Protestantism, however. When new movements and denominations arose, they were often subjected to significant popular and highbrow scrutiny; they were allowed to exist, by law, but this did not spare them from criticism and, on occasion, something very close to prosecution. It is also crucial to point out that political figures often joined in the chorus of disapproval.

Some fledgling denominations and movements—one might cite the Unitarianism and Transcendentalism of New England—suffered little more than onerous, rude remarks and scathing editorials in the press. Indeed, the first of these novel religious movements quickly secured a foothold in the religious sympathies of educated Bostonians. Transcendentalism, an offshoot of the Unitarian experiment, fared rather less happily. Ralph Waldo Emerson and Theodore Parker were never in danger of suffering at the stake or of languishing in prison, but some of their contemporaries lavished harsh criticism on them: an indication that a constitutional right to religious freedom did not signal a commitment to undiluted religious pluralism.

Others testified to this trend. A group such as the United Society of Believers in Christ's Second Appearing, better known as the Shakers, or Utopian experiments such as the Oneida community would scandalize much orthodox opinion, and for some members of these movements, the notion of unbridled religious freedom must have seemed more like a theoretical construct than a lived reality. Others, such as the adherents of William Miller and the Seventh-Day Adventists, would win converts from the Congregational, Presbyterian, Methodist, and Baptist communities with their talk of an imminent return of Christ. Some, such as Alexander Campbell, would call for a return to New Testament purity and a rejection of the debilitating internecine conflict that raged between competing Christian sects. All would suffer stigmatization.

Perhaps the most conspicuous example of inherent resentment toward new variants of Protestantism is provided by the experiences of the churches founded or continued by 19th-century African Americans.

## AFRICAN AMERICAN CHRISTIANITY

The people dragged to the Americas as slaves (and, here, we include present-day South America and the Caribbean) brought their own religious sensibilities with them. Plantation life was rarely conducive to the survival of their devotions, but as various archaeological and cultural remains bear testimony, they clung on regardless. In theory, the black slave was often expected to abandon his former religious identity and embrace Christianity, but in all manner of covert and inventive ways—dance, ritual, music, spirituality, rival pantheons, the blending of the old and the new—ancient practices and ideals were kept alive. We still see the signs of this ancestry, courtesy of the indubitable syncretism embedded in much African American religion and, more explicitly, in the modern-day practitioners of religious traditions such as Santeria and Voodoo—faiths, as we see in the next chapter, that would provoke their own debates about religious freedom and Church–State relations. It is also worth noting (not least because it is sometimes overlooked) that a sizeable proportion of the early-US black population had arrived from Islamic regions in Africa.

During the 19th century, however, Christianity, for better or worse, was the faith destined to have the greatest impact on the African American population, both slave and free. The unthinking, often brutal conversion efforts of slave owners were sometimes very different to the evangelical message preached during and subsequent to the Great Awakening. There was sometimes also a determined effort to enforce a bowdlerized version of Christianity, in which themes of liberation were conveniently downplayed. Nonetheless, many African Americans embraced the Christian message, usually of a Protestant variety, and set about recasting it as they saw fit. Out of this melting point, one of the most dynamic American religious traditions emerged, one that still influences black communities across the nation.

Unfortunately, being an African American Christian, even one who had secured freedom from slavery, was rarely easy during the late 18th and early 19th centuries. Even those who dutifully attended weekly services were subjected to indignity and prejudice. Segregation was the rule of thumb, and black congregants were routinely expected to crowd together in a designated part of the church. In response, a host of black congregations began to assert themselves—in Petersburg, Virginia; in Savannah, Georgia; and perhaps most memorably of all, in Philadelphia.

Some of the black congregants of St. George's Church in Philadelphia grew heartily tired of having to sit in a segregated gallery during services. Two of them, Absalom Jones and Richard Allen, decided to strike out on their own,, and in 1787 they helped to establish the Free African Society. Choices still had to be made, however. Was it best to find a niche within an existing denomination or to establish a church of one's own? Jones took the former route, securing his estimable place in history as the first black minister of the Episcopal Church in 1804. Allen went further,, and by 1816, he had managed to establish the African Methodist Episcopal Church.

This undoubtedly was a success story. By the middle of the 19th century, the AMEC had almost two hundred ministers in almost 300 churches, ministering to more than 17,000 members. Similar good fortune attended the American Methodist Episcopal Zion Church, which was founded by Peter Williams Sr. and which became a major contributor to the abolitionist debate.

Unsurprisingly, these advances provoked alarm in some sectors of the white community. Various commentators argued that allowing black congregations to meet without white oversight was a recipe for disaster. Such observers were especially cognizant of the fact that such groups were often full-square behind the abolitionist cause. Black criticism of the existing churches—Frederick Douglass, for instance, declaimed that "the church and the slave prison stand next to each other . . . the church-going bell and the auctioneer's bell chime in with each other"—raised many eyebrows. It is woefully reductive to put things so simply, but early 19th-century African American Christianity had two urgent tasks. First, there was the provision of much-needed spiritual sustenance. Second, there was a dedication to making things better—to strike out for independence. It was the latter objective that caused most consternation. Allow black Christians to assemble as they chose, and so the dubious logic went, social chaos would result.

Nat Turner's 1831 slave rebellion was grist to this mill,, and in an extraordinary feat of racist stereotyping (even for its time), many 19th-century white Americans decided that unregulated African American Christianity was anathema. Occasionally there were specific measures that required the presence of a white minister at any black religious assembly. Just as often, there were attempts to impose supervision and regulation. In some locales (Baltimore being a good example), the autonomy of black congregations was achieved relatively quickly. More often, such trends were either flatly rejected or much attenuated: hence the widespread notion that African Americans should be trusted with catechism classes or other educational initiatives, but not with a right to preach. In St. Louis, for instance, the First African Church was established in the early 1820s, but it remained under white supervision until 1827. There were often retrograde steps. Black congregations in Huntsville and Mobile, Alabama, for example, had grown used to hearing black preachers, but in the tense atmosphere of the 1850s, local Baptist associations once more began imposing exclusively white preachers on pulpits. Crucially, the discriminatory measures were sometimes backed up not only by the fiats of religious organizations but also by local municipal legislation.

It was a story of fitful progress (and is one of the less well-studied episodes in America's encounter with religious freedom). The 2nd Baptist Church in Richmond, Virginia, offers a typical trajectory. In 1821 the first African

American was admitted to the church's membership, and by 1846, 51 black congregants had decided to separate and establish their own church. A building was erected (courtesy of the labor of black slaves), but as the times seemed to dictate, the church's first pastor, Jeremiah Porter, was white. Occasionally, black preachers were allowed to ascend to the pulpit (though always under the closest white scrutiny), and it was not until 1866 that the church secured its first black pastor, the wonderfully named Pleasant Bowler.

Happily, such a transformation was not uncommon during the Reconstruction era. Over the coming decades, fully independent black congregations (which had once been a rarity) began to spring up across the nation. The Baptist denomination, which, at least in the North, had long been in the vanguard of change, led the charge. Black Baptist publications emerged, and black missionary efforts (including those aimed at Africa) went from strength to strength. The southern half of the nation also underwent seismic shifts, with—to cite just two examples—the arrival of an independent black Lutheran congregation in Little Rock, Arkansas, and in 1870 the establishment of the Colored Methodist Episcopal Church (an appellation that changed, in 1954, to the Christian Methodist Episcopal Church).

\*\*\*

These were important struggles, but if American Christianity was a house divided—with often uncomfortable consequences for the nation's new ideals of religious freedom and cozy Church–State relations—the experiences of other minority groups were just as sobering. Being a different kind of Christian was one thing; being no sort of Protestant at all was quite another.

## JEWS

Ahead of the gloom, one thing should be made abundantly clear: The religious freedoms and protections offered by the First Amendment were a huge boon to members of every single American religious group. As never before, Catholics, Jews, those of dissenting Protestant affiliations, and a whole host of new religious denominations were legally entitled to go about their devotional business without molestation—at least in theory. And there was the rub. Theory was not always the same as practice.

It is no coincidence that members of non-Protestant or less conventional Protestant beliefs have always been among the most vocal advocates of Church–State separation. It allowed them to thrive, and this has done wonders for the rich diversity of American religious life. However, such groups have been so vocal precisely because they realize how fragile these new freedoms can be.

In our discussion of colonial America, we demonstrated that a variety of Protestant denominations (chiefly Anglicans and Congregationalists) set the tone for the future of American religion. By the 19th century, other groups— Baptists, Methodists, Quakers—had managed to secure a position of broad social acceptance. In the case of the Baptists, this would transform into cultural dominance in some parts of the Union.

This still left many religious groups on the margins, regardless of how ancient or well established they happened to be. The real test of America's new attitude to religious diversity was how it would treat them. It did not always cover itself in garlands.

First, there were those religious groups who had existed long before the American colonial adventure had even been embarked on. The next chapter focuses on the fortunes of Native American religion, which turned out to be one of the most sensitive subjects confronted by the 20th-century Supreme Court, but in what follows, our attention turns to two other age-old faith traditions: Judaism and Roman Catholicism. During the 19th century, both groups made extraordinary progress, but they also suffered moments of stigmatization, even persecution, that came close to making a mockery of America's claims of expansive religious freedom.

Second, there were the bold (if sometimes wayward) religious experiments that defined 19th-century American religiosity. For all the protections of the First Amendment, how would America respond when new, provocative groups began to inhabit their devotional landscape? New denominations such as the Mormons and the Jehovah's Witnesses (both treated in more depth in the next chapter) would test America's commitment to religious freedom and force it to analyze the precise nature of Church–State separation.

***

The first chapter in American Jewish history did not begin well. In 1654, 23 Sephardic Jews arrived in New Amsterdam. We have already seen how the sitting governor, Pieter Stuyvesant, was committed to stamping out religious diversity,, and initially, he endeavored to prevent members of a "repugnant race" from settling in the colony. Luckily, he was overridden by the directors of the Dutch West India Company back in Holland. A few years later, another 15 Jewish families arrived in the more hospitable refuge of Rhode Island, and their descendants would go on to erect the Touro Synagogue (America's oldest) in 1763.

Throughout the colonial period the Jewish population in America was tiny (perhaps 2,000 souls at the time of the revolution). Jews were often allowed to trade and worship openly, although they were often still excluded from any role in political life and (just like members of dissenting Christian denominations) were usually expected to contribute through their taxes to the upkeep of established Christian churches. During this period there were sporadic instances of anti-Jewish violence, but for the most part, colonial anti-Semitism was limited to ostracism and the circulation of insulting Jewish stereotypes.

The constitutional settlement promised to usher in better days for American Jewry. In theory, Jews now stood on an equal civil footing with their Christian neighbors at the federal level. In various states, however, many of the old prejudices and disadvantages were slow to disappear, and as late as 1820, only seven of the original states had adopted constitutions that recognized Jews politically. In Maryland in 1826, for instance, legislation was proposed that would finally allow Jews to participate in the state's political process. Throughout the ensuing debate, familiar arguments were rolled out that insisted on the idea that the United States was, fundamentally, a Christian nation.

This concept was clearly challenged (one might even say made to look absurd) by the expansion of the Jewish population during the 19th century. By 1860 there were as many as 150,000 Jews in America, a figure much boosted by the influx of Ashkenazi Jews from central Europe. Nineteenth-century Judaism faced many problems. There were heated debates between those of orthodox and reformist sympathies and about the desirability of cultural assimilation. One thing that many Jewish leaders of different stripes agreed on, however, was that the religious and political freedoms of the new Republic held out great potential.

Some of them, especially within the Reformed fraternity, saw America as Zion and the Constitution as the fulfillment of mosaic principles. One very influential Jewish leader, Isaac Mayer Wise, wrote that Moses had long ago "promised the unsophisticated principles of democracy, liberty, and stern justice in an age of general despotism and arbitrary rule." As such, Moses "formed one pole and the American the other of an axis around which revolved the political history of thirty-three centuries."

Things were looking up, and Wise avidly studied America's history, visited its monuments, and mastered its language. He declared in 1869 that the United States was "the favoured high priestess of the goddess of liberty, with the diadem of honour and the breast place of justice." For all his boundless optimism, however, Wise remained acutely aware that Judaism still faced many obstacles and that longstanding prejudice still ran rampant.

Wise was deeply concerned about the inroads Protestant evangelism was trying to make into Jewish hearts and minds. Throughout his career he would denounce those Christian missionaries who sought to make Jewish converts, and in his efforts to undermine such people, Wise confessed that he had sometimes been obliged to become a "malicious, biting, pugnacious . . . monster of the press." The argument was simple: why couldn't Jews be left alone to follow their millennia-old religious path?

Wise reacted with outrage whenever public figures made anti-Semitic utterances. When one New York minister did just that in 1859, Wise launched a withering attack on the anti-Jewish fanaticism which "raises up its serpent head to the heavens . . . and spits its venom on those who unfortunately differ with it on religious views." When government became involved (surely a breach of Church–State separation) Wise was simply appalled. During the Civil War, for instance, he bitterly attacked the proposed ban on Jewish and Catholic chaplains in the armed forces and fumed against General Grant's infamous General Order 11 to remove Jews from areas under his control in December 1862.

As some of the subsequently expelled Jews explained to President Lincoln, they felt "insulted and outraged by this inhuman order, the carrying out of which would be the grossest violation of the Constitution and our rights as good citizens under it." As assaults on Church–State separation went, Grant's infamous order was especially noxious and was swiftly revoked.

Wise also refused to accept any infringements of the protections the First Amendment offered to his fellow Jews. From the mid-1840s, for instance, there was much agitation within the Jewish community against measures that seemed to exclude Jews from their rightful place in local communities. One recurrent bone of contention was the punishment of Jewish merchants (whose religious scruples meant they had to close their stores on their Saturday Sabbath) for breaking Sunday trading laws. This was perceived as a "violation of their natural rights as citizens . . . guaranteed by the constitution against the enactment of any law favouring any religious denomination."

Wise also opposed all attempts to include, by means of an amendment, any mention of Christianity in the constitution and fumed against Christian instruction in public schools. In 1856 he strongly objected to the Ohio governor's Thanksgiving Proclamation because it invoked the *Christian* people of the state. As early as 1812, Jews in Charleston had resented a similar proclamation that blithely called on all *Christian* denominations to hold services of thanksgiving, but that completely ignored the existence of Jewish congregations: this, they said, was nothing less than "an indignity . . . to the whole Jewish nation." Forty years later, Wise said that the Ohio proclamation read like a medieval papal bull and declared, "We are honestly tired of protesting every year" against such "illiberal and unconstitutional proclamations."

So far as Wise was concerned, "the entire and complete separation of church and state appears so desirable a policy to us that we abhor the interference of religious ministers in political affairs." He was especially sensitive to gaps between the principle of separation and its less-than-consistent application.

He was not alone. In 1863 a Jewish leader from the other end of the spectrum, Isaac Leeser, criticized his fellow religionists for their overly sanguine attitudes. "Some good-natured persons," he began, "who do not watch closely the course of events, may not discover any thing very alarming in the occurrences which are daily developed before our eyes." They were idiotically confident that their rights were secure. After all, they lived in a land "where freedom is at home." They could proudly point to the "beautiful constitution, the work of that august assembly over which the father of his country, the model of rulers, Washington, presided."

They thought of themselves as the inheritors "of the wealth of liberty and equality which he helped to secure." And then there was the First Amendment, aimed at securing

all classes, whether they be numerous, counting their adherents by millions, or few, confined perhaps within the space of a single household, in the full enjoyment of their conscientious convictions, to worship or not, as they may feel inclined, without any one being empowered to coerce them to enter his church, contribute to its support; or do aught which they would not do voluntarily and of a perfect free will.

But was it really quite so simple? Was everything quite as safe and secure as it seemed? There was always a risk that people would desire "to intermeddle with what does really not concern them; and it seems that no constitutional restraints, no prudential considerations, no impulses of common sense, are able to keep them within the bounds which we have indicated." In other words, the law was not the same thing as the reality of 19th-century American life.

It was from this state of affairs that religious persecution, "in all ages," had gradually arisen, and opportunistic politicians had always been happy to exploit it. Perhaps American lacked the brutish demagogues of former time, but "we should not be surprised," Leeser continued, "if a latent sentiment inimical to Judaism were already existing, and that it would spread still farther." There were suddenly many more Jews in the country, Leeser explained, "thus attracting to them a good deal of public attention." There was also resentment that efforts to convert them to Christianity had, by and large, been a failure. It was little "wonder that a deep-seated prejudice has by degrees been implanted in the minds of many honest, though ignorant persons, who become horrified the more they discover the Jewish countenance multiplied before them." Grant's awful order had proven the point: it had surely shown that "notwithstanding the boasted progress of the age, we are still in bondage." The entire Jewish community had been treated with "medieval cruelty," and as important as revoking the order undoubtedly was, revocation ought not bring any great solace. "A simple revocation of a military order . . . is no pledge that it may not be renewed at the first fitting occasion, when it may be made to inflict yet greater injuries and indignities than has been done in the present instance."

With the major expansion of Jewish immigration from eastern Europe between 1880 and 1920, by which date the Jewish population had risen to almost 3.5 million, new tensions and rivalries emerged. And in the century after Wise's and Leeser's deaths, the Jewish community would do much to defend the religious clauses of the First Amendment through such organizations as the Anti-Defamation League, founded in Chicago in 1913 by the lawyer Sigmund Livingston. The League's mission was to attack stereotyping, conspiracy-theorizing, and discrimination in everything from employment to education, "to stop, by appeals to reason and conscience, and if necessary by appeals to law, the defamation of the Jewish people . . . to secure justice and fair treatment to all citizens alike." That this was necessary demonstrates that a halcyon age of religious pluralism had not yet arrived.

## CATHOLICS

Living in a de facto Christian nation was sometimes very difficult for members of the Jewish faith, and living in a de facto Protestant nation did not always prove to be an easy wicket for Roman Catholics. As noted previously, colonial America had seen some rare instances (most notably in Maryland) during which Catholics were granted freedom of worship. It was far more common, however, for Catholics to face disadvantages and disenfranchisement. When Massachusetts enacted its revised charter in 1692, for instance, it proclaimed that "there shall be a liberty of conscience allowed in the worship of God to all Christians (except Papists)." This was far from being an unusual exclusionary measure.

The age of revolution seemed to signal a brighter future for America's Catholics. They were deemed to have played a loyal role in fighting against the British, and it was impossible to forget that a Catholic nation, France, had played a starring role in securing victory during the revolutionary wars. The first generation of native Catholic bishops, starting with John Carroll of Baltimore, struck many onlookers as somehow authentically American. One of them, Bishop John England of Charleston, South Carolina, became the first Catholic clergyman to preach to Congress in 1826.

This was progress, but there were still many conspicuously anti-Catholic measures on the statute books of various states—New Jersey and New Hampshire would continue to exclude Catholics from holding public office until 1844 and 1876, respectively. For all this, there was still a sense that American

Catholicism's fortunes had been much improved by the arrival of the First Amendment.

This led American Catholics down theological routes that their European confreres did not always welcome. The Catholic faith had traditionally been the keenest advocate of close interaction between Church and State. In countries across Europe there was a centuries-long assumption that a strong Catholic church, supported by the political establishment, was the ideal to be pursued. Throne and altar were to be joined at the hip.

This possibility was clearly not available to American Catholics, and some of them—much to Rome's displeasure—began to argue that the separation of Church and State was not merely a useful political practice but also a theologically reputable goal. Such separation, they argued, was precisely what allowed American Catholics freedom of worship. During the 19th century (and into the 20th), such musings provoked many squabbles between the American branch of the Church and the Roman hierarchy. American Catholics would play major roles in the so-called Modernist and Americanist crises, during which those of progressive theological stances battled against the more conservative elements within the Church. Simply put, although the late 19th-century Roman establishment often worked hard to stem the tide of various contemporary theological and philosophical ideas (including the embrace of Church–State separation), others saw virtue in pursuing a host of innovative political and intellectual causes (historically based biblical criticism, rationalism, subjectivism, and many others). It often came down to either embracing the intellectual currents of the modern world or rejecting them, and although the American Catholic Church was itself much divided on such issues, these debates undoubtedly provided American Catholicism with much of its dynamism. Crucially, there was a widespread confidence that the constitutionally sanctioned separation of Church and State was a boon to the American Catholic cause.

Unfortunately, this confidence was sometimes much tested during the 19th century. American religious freedom must have seemed like a dead letter when angry Protestant crowds burned down an Ursuline convent in Charlestown in 1834; when savage anti-Catholic riots erupted in Philadelphia in 1844; or when the residents of Ellsworth, Maine, stoned the house of the Jesuit John Bapst in 1854 and then undressed the priest, tarred and feathered him, and railroaded him out of town. Nor was it always about acts of violence. Midcentury anti-Catholicism also had a habit of covering itself in the respectable-looking clothes of journalism, scholarship, and high politics.

Many scurrilous commentators raised the alarm against imaginary papal invasion forces; Charles Chiniquy claimed that the Jesuits were responsible for both the outbreak of the Civil War and Lincoln's assassination, and Lyman

Beecher expressed his horror at the sight of Catholic missionaries evangelizing in the nation's western territories. In 1849 Charles Allen would organize his Order of the Star Spangled Banner out of which a national Know-Nothing party would emerge. Standing on a violently anti-Catholic, xenophobic platform—with its followers pledging never to vote for a Catholic, seeking to rob Catholics of all political influence, and campaigning to remove foreign-language instruction from public schools—the Know-Nothings grew enormously powerful in New York and Massachusetts state politics and secured dozens of congressional seats.

Much anti-Catholic sentiment suggested that the aims and beliefs of Catholicism were wholly incompatible with the democratic spirit of the new Republic. Whereas America stood for liberty, progress, and pluralism, Rome, Catholic bashers suggested—with its fondness for papal infallibility and its vigorous denunciations of the sins of the modern world—represented despotism and backward-looking obscurantism. Nineteenth-century anti-Catholicism was also about the hatred of immigration, about the xenophobic reaction to the influx of Catholic Irishmen during the worst years of the potato famine in the 1840s and 1850s.

Samuel Morse (1791–1872), famous for his code, did as much as anyone to popularize the notion that the Catholic monarchies of Europe were deliberately striving to undermine American institutions and morality by encouraging mass immigration. After fine-tuning his noxious anti-Catholic feelings during visits to Europe, Morse returned home; established a newspaper intended to alert Americans to the perils of popery; and warned, in his 1835 tract *Imminent Dangers to the Free Institutions of the United States through Immigration,* of the "great mass" of immigrants who, with their dead minds, were nothing but "senseless machines"—"they obey orders mechanically . . . they obey their priests as demigods . . . they have bee taught from infancy that their priests are infallible." Such people could never have their minds "illuminated to discern the nice boundary where their ecclesiastical obedience to their priests ends, and the civil independence of them begins."

Morse believed that "popery is opposed in its very nature to Democratic republicanism: and it is, therefore, as a political system as well as religious, opposed to civil and religious liberty, and consequently to our form of government." According to Morse, Catholicism was "spreading itself into every nook and corner of the land; churches, chapels, colleges, nunneries and convents, are springing up as if by magic everywhere." Priests were influencing elections; they had established so-called benevolent societies in order to efficiently organize the Catholic vote, and they had even tried to set up Catholic military forces. These were the simple "facts," Morse declared, and "if they are not facts they will be easily disproved."

*** 

In addition to defending against rabid polemics, American Catholics also had specific policy issues to confront. No Church–State debate has raised its head more often in America than the role of religion in public education. It is perhaps the most contested issue at the dawn of the 21st century, and it was headline news back in the middle of the 19th as well. Once again, New York provides a useful example.

Since 1805 the state's Public School Society had exerted significant influence over the curricula and organization of New York's schools: such was its remit. Some of its recommendations did not impress the city's Catholic population, however. In 1840 it decided to speak out against the society's approval (even encouragement) of the use of the Protestant King James Bible, of textbooks that portrayed the Catholic Church in an unflattering light, and of works of fiction in which stereotypical images of Irish immigrants as debauched social parasites were commonplace.

The eight Catholic parish schools in the city asked if, in the light of the anti-Catholic ethos that so many Catholic children had to endure, the Public School Society would provide them with a share of the funding (raised from general taxation) it had at its disposal. The petitioners made a basic, perfectly reasonable point: they were bearing their portion of the common burden by paying their taxes, but they were not allowed to participate in every common benefit. So far as common school education in New York was concerned, this participation had "been denied them for years back," except on

conditions with which their conscience, and, as they believe their duty to God, did not, and do not leave them at liberty to comply . . . Your petitioners only claim the benefit of this principle in regard to the public education of their children. They regard the public education which the state has provided as a common benefit, in which they are most desirous and feel they are entitled to participate; and therefore they pray your honourable body that they may be permitted to do so without violating their conscience.

In the city's public schools, Catholic children were being forced to read Protestant bibles and literature with a decidedly anti-Catholic tinge, and this could not be allowed to stand. Might it not be fairer to earmark some of this public taxation and allow Catholics to spare their children such indignities? The membership of the Public Society, they admitted, was composed of people belonging to various sects, including even one or two Catholics, and it certainly *claimed* to exclude all sectarianism from its schools.

If that claim proved to be false, however, and if "they do not exclude sectarianism, they are avowedly no more entitled to the school funds than your petitioners, or any other denomination of professing Christians." And what many people simply referred to as "religion" was actually, to a Catholic audience, patently sectarian and discriminatory.

Even the reading of scripture in those schools your petitioners cannot regard otherwise than as sectarian; because Protestants would certainly consider as such the introduction of the Catholic scriptures, which are different from theirs, and the Catholics have the same ground of objection when the Protestant version is made use of . . . many of the selections in their elementary reading lessons contain matter prejudicial to the Catholic name and character. The term "popery" is repeatedly found in them. This term is known and employed as on of insult and contempt towards the Catholic religion, and it passes into the minds of children with the feeling of which it is the outward expression. Both the historical and religious portions of the reading lessons are selected from Protestant writers, whose prejudices against the Catholic religion render them unworthy of confidence in the mind of your petitioners, at least so far as their own children are concerned.

Ultimately, the funds the Public School Society dispensed were raised by the taxing of New York's citizens, but why should Catholics contribute to something so manifestly detrimental to their interests? Catholics had the option of setting up their own institutions, of course, but they were still expected to pay their local taxes: "the expense necessary for this was a second taxation, required not by the laws of the land but by the no less imperious demands of their conscience . . . They were reduced to the alternative of seeing their children growing up in entire ignorance, or else taxing themselves anew for private schools." The solution was simple:

Should your honourable body be pleased to designate their schools as entitled to receive a just proportion of the public funds which belong to your petitioners in common with other citizens, their schools could be improved for those who attend.

The petition was rejected, but one very notable New York Catholic, Archbishop John Hughes, now joined the fight.

*** 

Hughes had long been a champion of Catholic rights and an opponent of anti-Catholic sentiment. Earlier in his career, in Philadelphia, he had debated with the Presbyterian John Breckinridge. The underlying anti-Catholicism of the early Republic and the determined Catholic attempt to prove that they posed no threat to civil and political order both came into the sharpest focus.

Breckinridge, in one of the 12 debates that took place, aimed his sights at the "coarse and ill-bred impertinence of a priesthood whose temper and treatment toward other men alternate between servility to their spiritual sovereigns and oppression of their unhappy subjects." In response to Breckinridge's horrifying stories of the crimes of the Inquisition and the enduring relationship between Rome and the world's worst despots, Hughes offered the most personal account of his own history. He recounted the death of his sister back in Ireland during his childhood. The law had made it impossible for the local Catholic priest to enter the churchyard and oversee the burial. All that was left to a grieving brother was to pick up a handful of dirt, have the priest bless it outside the churchyard, and scatter it on his sister's coffin.

It was to avoid such tragedies, Hughes informed his opponent, that his family had made the long journey to America. Rather than being an enemy of American ideals, he knew the full value of the civil and religious liberty that "our happy government secures for all." America, Hughes insisted, was a beacon and a haven for Catholics such as himself, a country in which no stigma would be impressed on his brow simply because he preferred one creed over another. Far from being a dangerous fifth column, Catholics were among the most loyal citizens the Republic had ever known.

This message would be reiterated by Hughes whenever his enemies called his patriotism into doubt. When two of his newspaper-owning critics did just that in New York, he was quick to act. Never in his life, he bellowed, had he done or said anything to rob anyone of the rights he claimed for himself under the Constitution. He had never "entered into intrigue or collusion" with a political party or an individual, and throughout his New York career, he had never done or said anything "unworthy of a Catholic bishop and an American citizen."

The New York schools issue was just Hughes's sort of fight. Was it not obscene, he asked, that Catholics were paying taxes so that their religion could be denounced in the ears of their children? A renewed petition was submitted, and at a public meeting in October 1840, Hughes made the Catholic argument in a speech lasting a full three hours. Ultimately, the petition was again rejected, but in 1841 Hughes had the idea of assembling a slate of candidates in the upcoming local elections who would campaign on the issue of public schools. They had limited success but made sufficient impact to seriously reduce the Democrat share of the vote. In 1842 a much-transformed New York legislature, now filled with suitably chastised Democrats, enacted legislation that established an elected Board of Education and prohibited sectarian religious education in the city's public schools.

This was a compromise that Hughes was willing to accept—it seemed to be the only workable way to expunge anti-Catholic aspects of the curriculum—but ultimately it was not an ideal solution for a Roman Catholic prelate. The notion of an education lacking in any religious content was not desirable.

Moreover, although the monopoly of the Public School Society had been removed, the state's school boards retained an undeniably Protestant identity, and all efforts to secure a share of public funding for Catholic schools met with failure. Over the next decade, Hughes would come to the conclusion that the Church's best alternative was to develop its own system of parochial schools, where Catholic children could be properly exposed to good Catholic doctrine. When the issue of readings from the King James Bible in public schools was raised once more, Hughes simply avoided involvement in the debate. As he explained, priorities had changed, and it was now vital to build schools first and churches second: "build your own schools," he urged his flock, and "raise arguments in the shape of the best educated and most moral citizens of the republic."

The battle over New York's public schools was not an isolated incident. The anti-Catholic violence that flared in Philadelphia in 1844, for instance, was a response to Bishop Francis Patrick Kenrick's efforts to protect the consciences of those Catholic students in common schools who had been expected to endure readings from the King James Bible. For the rest of the century, the issues of religion in public schools and funding for parochial schools would continue to be debated.

Whenever the Know-Nothing party gained political ascendancy, it invariably sought to use its influence to hinder the work of Catholic educators. In Massachusetts an amendment to the state constitution was proposed that forbade the provision of any public funds to sectarian schools, and little effort was made to disguise the anti-Catholic sentiment behind the measure: "If gentlemen say that the resolution has a strong leaning towards Catholics, and is intended to have special reference to them, I am not disposed to deny that it admits of such interpretation. I am ready to say to our fellow Catholic citizens: You may come here and meet us on the broad principles of civil and religious liberty, but if you cannot meet us upon this common ground, we do not ask you to come."

By the mid-1870s, James Blaine of Maine, also fired by anti-Catholic sentiment, was proposing an amendment to the national constitution that outlawed the provision of any public funds to sectarian schools. The amendment fell, but similar measures were enshrined in the constitutions of the majority of the states. It remains something of an irony that these pieces of legislation, with their unhappy origins in anti-Catholic bigotry, are made use of today by principled advocates of State–Church separation.

In Ohio the issue of religion in the public schools once more won national attention. John Baptist Purcell, bishop and later archbishop of Cincinnati, was a lifelong friend of John Hughes, and the two men regularly sought one another's counsel on a variety of pastoral and social issues. From the 1830s through to the 1860s, the issue of religion in Cincinnati's public schools was debated time and again, and various proposals—for example, allowing Catholic children to be excused from readings of the King James Bible and allowing Catholic children to read from their own bibles—were suggested.

Purcell had asked Hughes to visit him to discuss the issue or, failing that, to send him "a copious letter containing the necessary suggestions" to bolster the Catholic cause. In his reply, Hughes offered a very bleak analysis of efforts to reconcile Protestant and Catholic interests.

The Protestants' enmity to Rome is their great overruling passion, which they are willing to gratify in every degree, and by every means. With this conviction on my mind, you will not be surprised that I have no confidence in their religious friendship; that I dread their favors . . . In these coalitions there is no advantage. If we join them for instance in education, they will not expunge their abominable books. And if they should yield to correct some things, they will retain others. What has been excluded will be more than compensated by the implied sanction of what will be retained.

This was a depressing conclusion, but Purcell and other Catholic leaders were not entirely deterred from reaching some compromise. The debate continued, and in 1869 a bold proposal was discussed by the city's board of education. It was suggested that the Catholics should merge their schools with those of the board. To make this more palatable, it was proposed that all Bible-readings and religious instruction should be prohibited: "the true object and intent of this rule [was] to allow the children of the parents, of all sects and opinions in matters of faith and worship, to enjoy alike the benefits of the common school fund." Ultimately, the Catholic representatives withdrew from the discussions, but the proposed ban on Bible reading and religious instruction still had to be decided on by the board. A fierce debate—the so-called Ohio Bible War—ensued. The adherents of all major faiths, Jews as much as Protestants and Catholics, took up their positions. Meetings were held, and editorials were written, and when the board agreed to the ban, a legal action to gain an injunction was launched.

Defenders of the ban made many a rousing speech: it was suggested by one participant that the very notion that America was a Christian nation was really a sham, and another supporter of the ban rested his case on the fact that all he wanted was "to bring the children of Protestants, Catholics, Jews—yea, of unbelievers—together in the common school." First a temporary and then a permanent injunction was granted by the Cincinnati Superior Court, but in 1873 this was overturned on appeal by the Ohio Supreme Court, and the board's right to enact the ban on Bible reading and religious instruction was upheld.

The incident revealed much about contemporary views on Church–State relations and the place of the Roman Catholic Church in American society. Least edifying of all was the virulent anti-Catholicism that erupted when the ban was first proposed. There was also familiar talk about the dangers of letting religion disappear entirely from the public forum and of the disastrous consequences this would have for the nation's moral climate. At a meeting at Pike's Music Hall in September 1869, one speaker feared that the ban

means . . . not merely the exclusion of the Bible, but the expurgation, from every text book in the common schools, of every religious sentiment. It means the abolition, from the text books of the schools of Cincinnati, of every recognition of Christianity, or God Almighty, or conscience, or of accountability to the Supreme Being. It means to put it in a single sentence to make the schools of Cincinnati schools of atheism. And I say, my fellow citizens, that it is the most outrageous and damnable proposition that has ever been made in respect to our common schools.

Another speaker warned his audience of a "coalition which now seeks to expel the Bible from our public schools," and if they succeeded "in the real object which they are gradually coming at, the crushing out of all religious instruction, what will be the result?" he asked. "Who does not see that righteous men of all sects and creeds will then unite to tear down such a system. It will be far better, as one of the parties in this scheme proclaims, to have no public schools at all, than that they should be the 'godless' institutions which they would thus become." Those familiar with present-day debates over the place of religion in the public schools will perhaps be struck by how extraordinarily familiar some of those words and sentiments seem.

## MORMONS

Of all the novel religious groups that emerged during the 19th century, it was the Church of Jesus Christ of Latter-day Saints, better known as the Mormons, who perhaps enjoyed the most colorful and turbulent history. It is not hard to see why Mormon ideas caused so much controversy. They believed that the Book of Mormon, as dictated by their founder Joseph Smith, enjoyed the same status as the Old and New Testaments. It was seen as the fulfillment of earlier prophecies, of the "sealed book" mentioned in Isaiah, and nothing less than the final dispensation of the Almighty. Moreover, the book told of a millennia-long history during which Christ himself had visited the Americas. Smith was undoubtedly a dynamic and self-confident leader, a self-styled beneficiary of visions and angelic visitations who saw himself as the true inheritor of the authority of the ancient priesthood. He announced himself as the Church's prophet, seer, translator, and first elder, who would help his followers prepare for the imminent Second Coming.

It can also be stated with certainty that the early Mormons were a decidedly curious and exclusivist group. But as provocative as their theorizing might have been, it is still astonishing to recount just how much the Mormons had to endure during the 19th century. Their trajectory was a westward one, headed for some new settlement where they could await Christ's return. Wherever they went during the first decades after their foundation, Mormons were likely to receive a hostile reception. Smith himself would be tarred and feathered in March 1832, and spurious charges (from assault and battery to attempted murder) would regularly be made against Mormon leaders. The residents of Jackson County were unhappy with the Mormons' arrival. Violent clashes between locals and members of the Church ensued, and in the fall of 1833, the Church was driven out.

A little later, in Caldwell County, Missouri, the populace became resentful of the Mormons' presence (especially after members of the Church—voting en masse—had looked likely to influence the outcome of local elections). In October 1838, pitched battles between Mormons and locals began to erupt, culminating in a 250-strong mob shooting 20 Mormons dead (the "Haun's Mill Massacre"). Crucially, this took place just days after Governor Lilburn Boggs had ordered the Church to leave the territory: the "Mormons must be treated as enemies and must be exterminated or driven from the state, if necessary, for the public good. Their outrages are beyond all description." There were few signs of Church–State separation in such a remark.

Joseph Smith's engagement with politics also ended badly. In 1844, when he announced his intention to enter the 1844 presidential race, local Whig and Democratic politicians—realizing that they would now have to abandon hope of securing the Mormon vote—entered the ranks of Smith's enemies. By April 1844, dissenters within Mormon ranks had established a newspaper and a reformed Church of their own. The town council of Nauvoo (the Mormons' latest stopping point on their westward journey), headed by mayor Joseph Smith, declared that the newspaper was a public nuisance and closed down its presses. As a result, Smith was arrested in June. He was taken to Carthage jail, and on June 27, a mob with blackened faces stormed the prison and murdered Smith and his brother Hyrum.

The Mormons themselves were more than capable of moments of intolerance and outright violence (some of them savage) when dealing with their enemies. Romanticizing their odyssey is a mistake. It can be said with some justice, however, that the amount of derision and persecution that the Mormons faced was a sad reflection on contemporary American attitudes toward religious freedom. So far as Church–State relations were concerned, it is vital to realize that, more than once, the anti-Mormon charge was led by elected politicians and officials.

The Mormons were not slow to identify the indignities and insults they had to endure. In 1839, John Green travelled to Cincinnati to recount the outrages suffered by his brethren. The Mormons did not care whether people agreed with their beliefs, he explained. They were content if everyone thought their doctrines were evil, but the bloody events in Missouri were not about theology; they were about the contravention of basic American rights.

Fellow citizens . . . Turn not a deaf ear to this cry of the oppressed! The Mormons are outlawed, exiled, robbed . . . they ask of your justice and your charity that you befriend them. They have suffered these outrages from mob violence; they bid you beware, lest licentiousness unreproved bring ruin to your own privileges. Law has been trampled down, and liberty of conscience violated, and all rights of citizenship and brotherhood outraged by the house-burnings, field-wastings, insults, whippings, murders, which they have suffered; and in the name of humanity and of heaven, they pray you to utter the indignant condemnation merited by such crimes.

He had a point. There was a sustained campaign during the 19th century to blacken the Mormons' name. One alarmed citizen pleaded,

Citizens of the United States . . . arouse from your slumbers, for the enemy of truth is abroad in the land. Our beloved country is overrun with the propagators of the most mischievous delusion that has been recorded since the creation of man; and the consequence is that thousands are annually embracing it.

And one 1850s journal article explained,

One of the most striking features in the history of modern fanaticism is unquestionably the progress of Mormonism in the United States. That an uneducated youth, without the recommendation of decent morality, and in fact notorious only for a vagrant and dissolute life, should create and excite a new and revolutionary movement in the religious world, and be able to operate on the public mind by means of the most absurd pretences to the divine and prophetic character, and that too in an age and amongst a people who boast of their general intelligence, is a paradox scarcely to be accounted for on any known laws of the human mind.

The Mormons' solution was to head even further to the West, to territories outside the Union. There next followed what the historian Richard Bushman has aptly described as a "forty year battle between the Church and the US government." Mormon theocracy was seen as the antithesis of the American dream, and at one stage, in 1857, James Buchanan would go so far as sending armies to seize Mormon territories.

***

There was also one more very important controversy to play out: one that marked an important moment in the way Church–State relations were dealt with by the nation's courts. It centered on the Mormons' controversial support of the practice of polygamy. The Morrill Act of 1862 introduced new punishments for individuals convicted of bigamy. Unfortunately, it was often hard to prove that people had taken part in ceremonies that made polygamists of them, so most convictions relied on demonstrating the crime of bigamous cohabitation. There was therefore nothing exceptional in the conviction of George Reynolds, a Utah Mormon.

The trouble was, Reynolds had been given permission by his Church to have more than one wife: more than that, his Church suggested that failure to do so might have perilous consequences for his eternal soul. Here was a quandary. How were an individual's rights to exercise his religious freedom to be reconciled with the state's need to uphold the law of the land. In the Supreme Court case of *Reynolds v. United States* in 1879, Chief Justice Morrison Waite offered this answer:

Polygamy has always been odious among the northern and western nations of Europe, and until the establishment of the Mormon church was almost exclusively a feature of life of Asiatic and of African people. At common law the second marriage was always void and from the earliest history of England polygamy has been treated as an offence against society.

It was an example that the United States eagerly followed: "it may safely be said [that] there never has been a time in any state of the Union when polygamy has not been an offence against society, cognizable by the civil courts."

Claims of religious freedom could be pushed too far. Marriage was a civil contract and, therefore, very much within the purview of government. "Upon it society may be said to be built, and out of its fruits spring social relations and social obligations and duties with which government is necessarily required to deal." "It is impossible to believe," Waite suggested, "that the constitutional guarantee of religious freedom was intended to prohibit legislation in respect to this most important feature of social life."

If polygamy was to be allowed in order to salve individuals' consciences, what would come next? "Suppose [a person] believed that human sacrifice were a necessary part of religious worship, would it be seriously contended that the civil government under which he lived could not interfere to prevent a sacrifice?" A person could *believe* absolutely anything he wanted, but in the name of social order, there sometimes had to be limits to how he could *act*.

The 1880s saw an escalation in the campaign to stamp out Mormon polygamy, and at least 1,300 members of the Church subsequently spent time in jail. The Edmunds Act of 1882 forbade polygamists from serving on juries, excluded them from public office, and removed their right to vote. Five years later, the Edmunds-Tucker Act effectively disincorporated the Mormon Church and authorized the seizure of real estate not used for religious purposes. Faced with such pressures, the Church's president, Wilford Woodruff, acting for the "temporal salvation of the Church," ended the Mormon commitment to plural marriage. In a sense, the dream of a self-governing Zion was at an end. Like everyone else, Mormons were citizens of a territory (which became a state in 1896) that was ruled according to the rubrics of state and federal law.

Over the next century and a half, the issue raised by a member of Joseph Smith's fledgling church—the balance between religious freedoms and the social good—would come to dominate debates about the nature and limits of free exercise and about when and how the state should intrude on the actions of a religious organization. As we are about to see, the arena for many such debates was the courts.

## SUGGESTED READING

On Story, see James, McClellan, *Joseph Story and the American Constitution* (Norman, OK, 1971); and R. Kent Newmyer, *Supreme Court Justice Joseph Story: Statesman of the Old Republic* (Chapel Hill, NC, 1985). And on struggles in the early Republic, see Mark Douglas McGarvie, *One Nation under Law: America's Early National Struggles to Separate Church and State* (DeKalb, IL, 2004).

On Judaism, see Leon Jick, *The Americanization of the Synagogue, 1820–1870* (Hanover, NH, 1976); Bertram Korn, *American Jewry and the Civil War* (Philadelphia, 1951); Michael Meyer, *Response to Modernity: A History of the Reform Movement in Judaism* (New York, 1988). And on Wise, see David Philipson and Louis Grossmann, eds., *Selected Writings of Isaac Mayer Wise* (New York, 1969); Sefton Temkin, *Isaac Mayer Wise: Shaping American Judaism* (New York, 1992).

For Catholicism and Hughes, see James M. O'Toole, *The Faithful: A History of Catholics in America* (Cambridge, Mass., 2008); Stephan Brumberg, "The Cincinnati Bible War (1869–1873) and Its Impact on the Education of the City's Protestants, Catholics, and Jews," *American Jewish Archives Journal* 54 (2004): 11–46; Richard Shaw, *Dagger John: The Unquiet Life and Times of Archbishop John Hughes* (New York, 1977).

On Mormonism, see Richard L. Bushman, *Joseph Smith and the Beginnings of Mormonism* (Urbana, IL, 1984); Douglas Davies, *An Introduction to Mormonism* (Cambridge, UK, 2003); Terry L. Givens, *The Viper on the Hearth. Mormons, Myths and the Construction of History* (Oxford, 1997); Klaus J. Hansen, *Mormonism and the American Experience* (Chicago, 1981); Kenneth H. Winn, *Exiles in a Land of Liberty. Mormons in America 1830–1846* (Chapel Hill, NC, 1989). The definitive biography of the Mormons' founder is Richard Lyman Bushman, *Joseph Smith: Rough Stone Rolling* (New York, 2005).

# 6

# To the Courts

The 20th century would bring many challenges. Some would be familiar. The relationship between Church and State is often conceptualized in terms of government either avoiding or embracing religious issues. It is, of course, a two-way street: we also have to consider the phenomenon of religious leaders becoming deeply involved in political matters. America has long-debated the rectitude of such activity, and there have been many flashpoints during which this has become an especially urgent question.

During the 19th century, the very political issue of slavery was often much-influenced by the deeds and opinions of churchmen. Some turned to the Gospel in order to advance the abolitionist cause. Others tried to dampen down the flames of change by insisting that religious leaders should keep out of politics. The Presbyterian minister James Henry Thornwell, irked by the abolitionist agenda, fell back on the notion of strict Church–State separation. The two spheres, he opined, should be seen as "planets moving in different orbits and unless each is confined to its own track, the consequences may be disastrous."

It is often supposed that separationism is a liberal, left-leaning monopoly. These days, it usually is. As Thornwell demonstrates, however, it could also be put to conservative and, in this instance, disreputable use. As already mentioned, the very state rules and regulations that prohibit religion from playing too conspicuous a role in public education (a contemporary liberal shibboleth) had their genesis in bilious 19th-century anti-Catholicism. That, as they say, is a paradox, but then the Church–State debate is full of them.

As for keeping priests and pastors out of politics, this was an unachievable, and probably wrongheaded, goal. The 20th century would witness many moments and movements during which church leaders energized policy debates. From Prohibition to the civil rights movement, they would be in the thick of things. Today, there are constraints: a minister whose church or organization enjoys tax exemptions is theoretically supposed (by IRS commandment) to stop short of direct endorsement of particular political candidates. As we all know, however, this is a rule that is often honored in the breach.

This is an old issue, but the 20th century also opened up new vistas and dilemmas. The notion of America being, at heart, a Christian nation became increasingly dubious (it had always been in jeopardy). Hinduism, Islam, and any number of alternative religious traditions gained welcome ground, and perhaps most puzzlingly for experts in First Amendment jurisprudence, so did those who believed in no God at all. Previously, a theistic consensus had ruled the roost; atheism made things much more difficult.

Atheists would play a momentous role in 20th-century debates about America's religious and cultural identity. They helped to add a new layer to the debate about faith and politics. Supporting an evenhanded attitude toward all religions was one thing, they suggested, but what about those who evinced no religious beliefs whatsoever? In this regard, the deeply controversial Madalyn Murray O'Hair emerged as a very significant figure. First motivated by her son having to witness acts of religious devotion at school, O'Hair helped to establish the American Atheists organization: a body that, to this day, regularly enters the arena of controversial politics. Recent years have seen atheist-leaning organizations launching protests against everything from NASA astronauts reading from the Bible while in space to a pope celebrating mass on federal ground in Washington, D.C.

If, as the pollsters tell us, principled non-belief is on the increase in the United States, then we can certainly expect to hear more from atheists in debates about the Church–State relationship.

The same prediction holds good for those of non-Christian and idiosyncratically Christian beliefs. On the latter front, America is occasionally torn asunder by the debate over what should count as a legitimate religious tradition: when is a cult a cult, and when is a faith a faith that warrants First Amendment protection? As testified to by the 1993 governmental intervention in events surrounding the Branch Davidians at Waco, Texas; the investigations into the Unification Church; and the curious history of the Church Universal and Triumphant in rural Montana, there are always likely to be controversial moments when those who wield political authority will be obliged to think long and hard about the intersection between religious freedom and the general rule of law.

As for other, non-Christian but well-established faiths, the ground can sometimes be equally slippery. American pluralism has, to its credit, allowed faiths such as Hinduism, Buddhism, Bahaism, and Islam to flourish, but such welcome developments carry their share of tricky issues in their wake.

There was mention earlier of the religious ideas that arrived from Africa during the slaving era. For the most part, such belief systems tended either to seek quiet anonymity during the 19th century or to satisfy themselves with acts of syncretism, profoundly influencing the identity of some varieties of African American Christianity. Today, religions such as Santeria (a fascinating hybrid of West African tradition and Cuban colonial experience) represent a proud and defiant presence on the American religious landscape.

Occasionally, Santeria's rituals provoke consternation in some quarters. Animal sacrifice, for instance, has a tendency to raise eyebrows, but as the Supreme Court has ruled, if an unusual practice is part and parcel of an established religion's devotional structure, and if it does not tangibly harm the public good, then, as the First Amendment indicates, it warrants protection against inequitable local laws.

The 1993 case of *Church of the Lukumi Babalu Aye v. City of Hialeah* made this clear. The case involved practitioners of the Santeria religion whose rituals included animal sacrifice. The group wanted to set up a settled place of worship within the city of Hialeah, Florida, but the city council issued ordinances that forbade the sacrificing of animals. A district court ruled that the ordinances were constitutional, a judgment confirmed by the Court of Appeals for the 11th Circuit. The Supreme Court, by contrast, ruled that the ordinances were unconstitutional. In this case, because the laws were neither neutral nor generally applicable, it was still necessary for the city council to prove that there was a compelling interest for enacting the laws or that there was no way that said interest could be achieved through less intrusive means. In his ruling, Justice Anthony M. Kennedy argued that the council had failed in both of these objectives. That is not to say, as recent events in Euless, Texas, where the issue of animal sacrifice within the Santeria faith once more hit the headlines, that the argument is over.

We can therefore be confident that the aspirations and demands of minority faiths are destined to shape the future direction of Church–State debates, but there is unlikely to be a more significant contributor to such arguments than a religion that has existed and flourished for many centuries: Islam.

## ISLAM

There have been many American Muslims for a very long time. They came as slaves from West Africa, as migrants from the Middle East, and, not least during the latter part of the 19th century, as converts. Islam managed to captivate the minds of many Americans. Mohammad Alexander Russell Webb, as he would come to be known, served as U.S. consul to the Philippines between 1887 and 1892 and journeyed home with Islam in his heart, converting to the faith and even serving as its representative at the Chicago World's Parliament of Religions in 1893. Even back in the Revolutionary era, extending religious freedom to Muslims was worn as a badge of pride by many of the architects of America's constitutional settlement. In his bill for Virginian religious freedom, Thomas Jefferson explicitly included the "Mahometan," and when Massachusetts drew up its state constitution, Muslims were, at least in principle, afforded "ample liberty of conscience."

It would be erroneous to suppose that American Muslims have not endured discrimination. They assuredly have, and as their numbers grew during the 20th century—largely as a result of determined evangelizing efforts—their fortunes, in terms of religious freedom, often worsened. From the 1930s onward, the African American Islamic constituency soared. The Nation of Islam movement, most especially under the leadership of Elijah Muhammad and Louis Farrakhan, adopted a provocative approach to American culture, often arguing for a stark division between the black Islamic community and what it perceived as an oppressive white establishment.

Such developments had radical implications for American Islam and its relationship with Church–State issues. In many important quarters, American politics were turned upside down. A new (or, at least, more well-defined) political constituency was created, and to this day, the rights of members of the Nation of Islam to assert their beliefs and read whatever literature they choose is, quite properly, a standard theme in First Amendment debate. Just as importantly, however, we should also recognize that the Nation of Islam, though dynamic, does not define the entire American Islamic experience. More orthodox and (by some definitions) less combative and more level-headed groups also exist. The common ground all Islamic groups share is the response of the non-Islamic majority, and this will doubtless become one of the 21st century's acid tests of America's commitment to religious freedom and scrupulous separation of Church and State.

In the wake of the 9/11 tragedies, a loathsomely stereotypical attitude toward Islam has developed within some byways (and, much more regrettably, in some of the main boulevards) of the popular American imagination. A far more sensible approach is to accept and relish the fact that in the first decade of the 21st century, there are something like 7 million law-abiding American Muslims, worshipping in 1,200 or so mosques around the country. That some Islamic worldviews differ from those of either the mainstream Christian Churches or the much-touted modern secularists is both inevitable and, tellingly, an opportunity. The challenge that lies ahead involves recognizing and respecting this theological gap.

So far, the signs are mixed. Some school districts include Muslim celebrations on their roster of public holidays, but contrariwise, the act of wearing the hijab has caused Muslim women much unnecessary trouble when, for instance, they try to serve as doctors or teachers; when they bear witness in a public courtroom; or even, farcically, when they attempt to cash a check at their local bank.

America has been here before: caught in this balance between respecting individual religious conscience and sustaining common order. It seems reasonable to suggest that allowing an employee to pray as often as his or her religion dictates or to wear whatever clothes he or she chooses does not represent an immediate threat to national security. How America deals with such concerns will, no doubt, help to define its reputation as a bastion of free expression.

But we are getting ahead of ourselves. The fundamental points are that, throughout the 20th century, America invited religious pluralism and that this, for all the subsequent headaches, might have been to its advantage. Back now to the brass tacks of history. With all the foregoing issues in mind, and with various surprises in store, how did America's jurists cope? It was a new religious landscape, brimful of rival faiths. Unsurprisingly, chaos sometimes diluted by common sense was regnant. And so to the courts.

## THE U.S. SUPREME COURT

The trends mentioned are extremely important, but an equally significant 20th-century development occurred when the Supreme Court finally stopped dipping its toe into the specific interpretation of the First Amendment and gave over a large proportion of its docket to the undertaking. We have already seen hints of this, and things would never be quite the same again.

\*\*\*

It was during the 1940s that the Supreme Court embarked on a determined campaign to apply the pronouncements of the Fourteenth Amendment to First Amendment religious jurisprudence. As soon as this hurdle was cleared, there was a veritable avalanche of legal proceedings that sought to tease out the true meaning of America's religious freedoms.

The Supreme Court has always been selective when it comes to deciding which cases to consider. It has sometimes received a less than adoring press because of this pick-and-choose attitude. Occasionally, the criticism has been richly deserved. In recent years, the Court has sometimes sought to avoid encounter with various explosive issues—school vouchers and the religious content of the post-1954 Pledge of Allegiance, for instance—but for the most part, the Court has relied on a tried and tested legal strategy. If the decision of a lower court does not appear to represent a flagrant abuse of a constitutional principle, then it makes little sense for the highest court in the land to revisit that decision. Allowing a lower court's ruling to stand and refraining from hearing an appeal is, in principle, a sensible way of proceeding. The docket is already crowded enough, so battles have to be picked carefully.

That this mechanism is occasionally abused in order to avoid controversy is clear for all to see, but on the whole, the Supreme Court has made sensible decisions about which cases to hear. And as any law student could tell you, it has certainly not been shy about taking on provocative cases in the realms of religious freedom and Church–State separation. Some have called the Court lazy; others have called it overly proactive. It can never win, and on balance, and for all the shifting judicial personnel and their often transparent political agendas, the Supreme Court has certainly taken these issues seriously.

The remainder of this book is dedicated to analyzing this long and winding legal history. It is important to realize, of course, that the Supreme Court is not the only venue where issues of Church and State are confronted. Less lofty tribunals also play an important role, and in what follows, mention will regularly be made of decisions in the various U.S. circuit courts. Also, many local battles simply never make it to the courtroom. School boards make their decisions about the introduction of creationist teaching, and religious posters or monuments spring up in public buildings; in short order, attentive organizations such as the ACLU or Americans United for Separation of Church and State lodge their protests, and quite frequently, matters are settled out of court.

These parochial controversies ought not be forgotten. In a sense, they represent the frontline of Church–State debate, and for the people concerned, they are presumably every bit as important as the legal rulings handed down by a federal courtroom. That said, there is no better way to trace America's broad approach to Church–State controversies than to sketch the meandering decisions of the Supreme Court over the past 60 years.

Those decisions have certainly not demonstrated consistency, and there have been several moments when members of the Court have overturned the decisions of their predecessors. Moreover, the divided decision, the all-too-familiar 5–4 split, has been far from uncommon in Church–State rulings. It is worth remembering, however, that it is not the business of the Supreme Court to handpick cases that allow for the straightforward elucidation of legal principles. By a very sensible mandate, it is there to respond to the claims of defendants and plaintiffs in very specific circumstances. This inevitably makes it harder to achieve either consistency or coherency, but there is no other legitimate way of proceeding. In general, the Court's justices deal first and foremost with the specifics of a particular case and then, in their rulings, often expand (sometimes wisely, sometimes oddly) their analysis to broader constitutional ideas.

During the past 60 years, it has been possible to identify shifting factions both within the Court and within the ranks of legal scholars who pore over their decisions. Some have adopted what is termed an "originist" approach, giving highest priority to following the aspirations of the Constitution's authors, whereas others have argued for a more organic strategy—using the words of the First Amendment as a springboard while paying at least as much attention to shifting historical circumstances. Some have been resolutely separationist, usually relying on the Jeffersonian wall metaphor, whereas others have grounded their thinking in an acceptance of the continued importance of religious belief to the American people. Meanwhile, the fashionable, well-intentioned notion of neutrality in Church–State affairs has come up against the arguments that (a) neutrality is impossible to achieve or (b) it can easily cross the line into hostility toward religion.

These and many other debates continue to rage, and the only safe conclusion is that, when confronted with the issue of Church–State relations, even the most brilliant of American legal minds have a tendency to differ. The controversy, in other words, is still alive and well.

***

When interrogating all the case law, it makes good sense to distinguish between the two aspects of the First Amendment's religion clauses. One of them speaks directly to religious freedom—the right to worship, think, and proselytize as you see fit. The other is chiefly concerned with governmental entanglement with religion. Naturally, most of our time here is spent analyzing Church–State cases. However, the two halves of the First Amendment's religion clauses cannot always be easily differentiated.

Church–State separation can exist at a basic, institutional level (a government can be prevented from sponsoring the interests of a specific religious faith, for instance), but a total division of political and religious issues is well nigh impossible. This is the paradox of the First Amendment. The amendment requires the state to preserve the religious freedoms of its people. This, by any standard, obliges the state to entangle itself with matters of faith, albeit from a supposedly impartial, entirely legal-minded perspective.

It therefore makes sense to spend a little time looking at the post-1940s cases in which the Supreme Court has attempted to define the nature of America's religious freedoms. This is a crucial aspect of Church–State relations, and perhaps more importantly, it reveals just how blurry the line between Church–State and religious freedoms cases has sometimes been.

## RELIGIOUS FREEDOM I

Ideally, the First Amendment would allow any American to believe and worship however he or she chooses. Ideally, the government and the courts would never have to get involved. Unfortunately, though perhaps inevitably, this optimistic vision has sometimes collapsed. Occasionally the exercise of an individual's religious freedom has been deemed to threaten or disrupt political and social order or the common good. This is an easy idea to grasp. Imagine, for instance, that members of faith X are obliged, according to the tenets of their religion, to steal from the local supermarket every Wednesday or throw rocks at their neighbor's house once every year. Quite obviously, such behavior would be seen as inappropriate—an obvious breach of general, secular laws—and even if an individual engaging in them claimed that his errant actions were a necessary part of his religious devotions, this would not protect him from prosecution or, at the very least, a state-led insistence that he cease and desist.

Mercifully, America has rarely confronted such absurd examples of how the right to religious freedom does not excuse socially disruptive behavior. The basic point remains the same, however. There are times when the exercise of religious freedom can pose a threat to the well-being, coherency, and smooth-running of society. Deciding what constitutes such a threat has been one of the chief tasks of America's courts. It has often come down to squaring the duty to allow people freedom of belief with the state's overriding duty to preserve order.

When the line is crossed, so the theory goes, the state is entitled to intervene and to set limits on the religious freedoms enjoyed by its citizens. We have already seen one example of this: the campaign against Mormon polygamy. With the dawn of the 1940s, another fledgling religious group brought such issues into both the headlines and, time after time, the federal courtroom. That group was the Jehovah's Witnesses, and as quirky as some of their doctrinal positions were, they did as much as any other religious tradition to define and codify the true meaning of the First Amendment.

***

Founded by the Pittsburgh merchant Charles Taze Russell in the last quarter of the 19th century, the Bible Students, known later as the Jehovah's Witnesses, have historically been a decidedly insular organization, openly, sometimes rabidly, critical of every other church and religious movement in human history. In a sense their role in defining and expanding America's understanding of religious freedom is paradoxical.

At the heart of Russell's theological vision was the absolute certainty that the return of Jesus Christ was imminent. Russell suggested that, in 1874, Christ had embarked on his "invisible" appearance, or *parousia*, and that the year 1910 would witness a swathe of global disasters leading up to Armageddon in 1914. Those who heeded Russell's message would join the 144,000 company of the elect, destined to rule with Christ in heaven. From the outset, Russell's Bible Students movement was intolerant of other faiths. It insisted on biblical fundamentalism and rejected many traditional Christian doctrines (the Trinity, for instance) and much of the apparatus of Christian worship (such as church buildings). It also demonstrated a strong evangelistic impulse, and this was precisely the tendency that brought it into the national Church–State spotlight.

The most dynamic, and most controversial, leader of the denomination during the first part of the 20th century was Joseph Franklin Rutherford: a man dedicated to autocratic power. One of the Bible Students' most famous causes was its refusal to provide military service to the state, a message reiterated throughout World War 1 and between the covers of Rutherford's book *The Finished Mystery.* Here was an early instance of the denomination's ability to raise issues that complicated Church–State relations. Did the Bible Students' right to religious freedom entitle them to denounce military service and the waging of a world war, or did the state have an obligation to silence such ideas?

At first, the latter argument won the day. The book was banned in Canada in 1918, and in the United States a campaign against the book culminated in the arrest of Rutherford and seven other board members under the terms of the American Espionage Act. As the arrest warrants put it, their actions had "unlawfully, feloniously, and wilfully caused insubordination, disloyalty and refusal of duty." Seven of the accused were sentenced to 20 years in prison (the eighth received a 10-year sentence), and for the next nine months they were incarcerated in Atlanta, Georgia.

In March 1919, the debate shifted gear when Supreme Court Justice Louis Brandeis ordered the release of the prisoners. The convictions were later reversed (owing to the lack of a "temperate and impartial" trial), and in 1920 the U.S. government withdrew all charges. It was only the beginning of the long and turbulent history of a movement that, from 1931, was known as the Jehovah's Witnesses.

One of the dominant themes of Rutherford's presidency was an increasingly rigorous separation from the institutions and customs of mainstream American life. It was a fundamental article of faith among the Bible Students that the fleshly, workaday world was the domain of Satan. Existing political organizations, churches, and the capitalist system were hopelessly corrupt and tarnished: quite literally the devil's work. Through the 1930s Rutherford urged his coreligionists to ignore political elections, to avoid such pagan customs as Christmas celebrations and birthday parties, and to play no role in the existing institutions, not just in the armed forces but also in unions, the scouts, and even parent–teacher associations.

This might suggest that the Witnesses would have been happy to squirrel themselves away in isolated communities and to let the rest of humanity go about their carnal business. But nothing could have been farther from the truth. Back in 1919 Rutherford had begun to publish the *Golden Age* for nonbelievers, and the Witnesses soon began to embark on extraordinarily energetic proselytizing efforts—going door-to-door in communities with their pamphlets, recordings, and other wares.

This was not always popular. In 1928, New Jersey Bible Students were accused of infringing local laws against disturbing the peace, against engaging in certain kinds of activities on Sundays, and against distributing literature without securing the appropriate licenses. In 1936, 1,149 Witnesses were arrested on such charges.

In the next few years a series of important cases tackled the question of whether the Witnesses' liberties were being infringed by the efforts of local communities to outlaw their evangelical activities. What counted most? The Witnesses' right to free exercise or the community's need to make them abide by general laws (such as securing trading licenses) and to prevent them from disturbing the peace? In 1940, in response to these very questions, a case came before the Supreme Court that would be remembered in legal annals as one of the most pivotal events in American judicial history.

\*\*\*

The case of *Cantwell v. Connecticut* centered on a Jehovah's Witness from New Haven, Newton Cantwell. As his determinedly evangelical faith demanded, he went door-to-door in his community peddling religious literature and, on occasion, playing a record that included attacks on the Roman Catholic religion. For many, this was an obvious example of the exercise of religious freedom overstepping the mark. Cantwell was convicted of breaching the peace (loudly insulting another religious group) and of soliciting funds without a license: everyone else had to secure such licenses, so why should this generally applicable law not apply to the member of a religious group?

The Supreme Court was not impressed by this analysis. It ruled that the Connecticut law that required Cantwell to obtain a license represented an infringement of his right to free exercise. Justice Owen J. Roberts, in a unanimous ruling, began by reiterating the mantra of the Reynolds Mormon case and the principle we have been discussing: in order to protect society, the state could sometimes regulate religious practices. In this instance, however, the state law was judged to be an unreasonable restraint on free exercise. Cantwell might have been perceived as a nuisance by many of his fellow citizens, but his activities did not pose an excessive threat to public order or policy.

This was a watershed ruling because, for the first time, it applied the religion clauses of the First Amendment to the states via the Fourteenth Amendment. The Connecticut law could not be allowed to stand because it violated the rights that Cantwell enjoyed as a citizen of the United States. This seemed to be a robust legal notion, and in fact, only three years later, another case, *Murdock v. Commonwealth of Pennsylvania,* allowed the Supreme Court to hammer home the point. Much like Cantwell, Robert Murdock and some of his fellow Witnesses had distributed religious literature in exchange for financial contributions. As a result, and again just as with Cantwell, they had been charged with breaching a law that forbade such solicitation without first acquiring an appropriate license. The Witnesses argued that the need to obtain such a license assaulted their basic right to freedom of speech, press, and religious exercise. In a 5–4 decision (significantly, a much closer call than the ruling in Cantwell), the Supreme Court upheld their argument.

If trading licenses was one thing, however, the nation's most prized and precious symbol was potentially quite another. In the same year as *Murdock,* the Witnesses once more came into the national spotlight, thanks to the case of *West Virginia State Board of Education v. Barnette.* America has always been obsessed with showing due, even excessive, reverence to its flag. Accordingly, in 1942, the West Virginia Board of Education resolved that it was now mandatory for all students to salute and pledge allegiance to the flag of the United States. Any students who refused to comply risked expulsion from school. Worse yet, this would result in such children being declared delinquent, and their parents would face the possibility of prosecution and even a custodial sentence. Patriotic fervor was running high when the education board enacted its resolution: it had been only a month since the Japanese attack on Pearl Harbor.

For all that, some Virginians found it impossible to force their children to salute the flag: for them, this was an unnecessary assault on their consciences. A group of Jehovah's Witnesses, including Walter Barnette, insisted that their faith taught them that the flag was a graven image and that making their children salute offended their religious scruples. The Supreme Court, basing its majority decision on the First Amendment's freedom of speech clause, agreed. Even in such straitened circumstances, coercively promoting patriotism (including threatening to expel children from school) was unconstitutional.

Technically, this case was adjudicated according to the rubrics of free speech, but Justice Robert Jackson found space to coin an enduring description of American religious freedom: "if there is any fixed star in our constitutional constellation, it is that no official, high or petty, can prescribe what shall be orthodox in politics, nationalism, religion, or other matters of opinion or force citizens to confess by word or act their faith therein."

But the Court was unified in its adjudication. In an important dissenting opinion, Justice Felix Frankfurter argued that a flag salute was a perfectly reasonable way to promote national unity and, by extension, national security. So far as Frankfurter was concerned, the refusal to salute the flag undermined the coherency and, one assumes, the morale of an embattled nation. Religious freedom or the right to free speech did not excuse an individual from supporting such causes.

In fact, Frankfurter is a good early example of a Supreme Court justice who, from his perspective, sought to limit supposed abuses of the free exercise clause. In one of those earlier Jehovah's Witnesses cases, he had insisted that just because a person was engaged in religious activity, this did not necessarily mean that they were exempt from commonplace taxation (the acquisition of a trading license, in that instance) that applied to every other member of the community. Where was the discrimination, he wondered? The licensing rubric applied to everyone, so why should it not apply to a religious group? As we'll see, this concept of enforcing a generally applicable law would have a bright future ahead of it.

*** 

The history of the Jehovah's Witnesses is something of a gift for students of the Supreme Court's approach to religious freedom. In a few short years their activities managed to expose the arguments and fault lines that would continue to divide legal opinion for the next several decades. The Witnesses are especially fascinating because they were, by any standard, a tricky denomination to confront. The freedoms that protected them were not necessarily freedoms that chimed with their own exclusivist theological vision. The notion of religious pluralism and tolerance was the farthest thing from their minds. Their importance should not be underestimated, however. For a few years during the early 1940s, they forced jurists to confront the consequences of the First Amendment's religion clauses in more detail than ever before.

More than that, they did so in a period (a world war, no less) when social cohesion was of paramount importance. The decisions of the Supreme Court during these years ought to be a source of pride for Americans. The particular outcomes are rather less important than the process. For everything that was going on around it, the Court worked very hard to focus on the pristine application of law. Puzzling over the First Amendment was hard enough; being distracted by the popular mood would have made things impossible. This was something that most, though not all, members of the Court realized.

In any event, the Witnesses had scored some memorable victories, though they did not enjoy carte blanche. Sometimes, according to the Supreme Court, they went too far. Just as World War II was heading toward a desirable conclusion, the 1944 case of *Prince v. Commonwealth of Massachusetts* came to Washington. Sarah Prince, a resident of Brockton, Massachusetts, had been arrested for allowing her nine-year-old niece to join her evangelizing efforts, including the distribution of Jehovah's Witness pamphlets. Prince was convicted for breaching a state law that forbade children from trading in public, but riding high on the wave of recent decisions, she averred that this was an infringement of her right to free exercise.

Much to Prince's dismay, this time around, the Supreme Court argued that the state law was constitutional. The Court stated that, first, there were occasions when the government could regulate religious activities in the public interest: the acid test that we have already spent some time discussing. In this instance, it was argued that allowing a child to sell pamphlets was an obvious case in point. Second, the Court suggested that even though the Massachusetts law limited the religious freedom of an individual, this was overridden by broader concerns. First, the individual in question was being stymied only in an indirect way (she could act as she chose; the Court was really responding only to the activities of her niece). Second, the law she was deemed to be breaking (putting a child to work, whatever the purpose) was not aimed at attacking religious freedom. It was a neutral law (that is, applicable to everyone) with a worthwhile secular purpose (preventing child labor).

Such notions (sometimes applauded, sometimes queried) would enjoy a lengthy period in the judicial sun over the next few decades. Tussles over when it was appropriate for the state to intervene in the exercise of religious freedom (which almost always meant limiting it) were set to continue. Given the parameters of this book, we have room only for a sketch.

***

Was it sensible for the state to insist on a uniform day of rest, for instance? On paper this made excellent sense: all shops would close their shutters on Sundays in order for no merchant to be placed at a disadvantage. Matters became more confusing when those of different, non-Christian faiths disagreed about which day ought to be cordoned off from commercial activity.

In 1961 the Supreme Court heard the case of *Braunfeld v. Brown*. This was an echo of the old 19th-century squabbles that had much concerned America's Jewish communities. Orthodox Jewish businessmen, including

Abraham Braunfeld, the proprietor of a clothing and furniture store in Pennsylvania, challenged local Sunday-closing laws that had been in place since 1959. For the soundest of reasons, the Jewish faith demanded that its followers close their stores on the Saturday Sabbath. Given the buying habits of the American public, this posed an obvious problem. In order to avoid financial disadvantage, Braunfeld and others opened their businesses on Sundays instead—making up for lost time, as it were—but this fell foul of the Pennsylvanian law.

Braunfeld argued that this interfered with the free exercise of his religion. His faith made it impossible to open up shop on a Saturday, so he was surely entitled to recoup lost profits by trading on a Sunday. To suggest otherwise would be prejudicial. The Supreme Court was not convinced by the argument, and with a 6–3 majority, it upheld the state law that forbade Sunday trading. In his majority decision, Justice Earl Warren argued that the law was not intended to prohibit a religious activity but rather to achieve a secular purpose: the establishment of a uniform day of rest.

This was certainly one of the shakiest of Supreme Court adjudications. The argument for putting social order and cohesion ahead of individual religious freedom has always been a good and entirely necessary one. But it remains unclear how preventing Jewish people from going about their business on a Sunday so that they could observe their age-old religious observances on a Saturday represented such a horrendous threat to social order.

Theoretically, Warren was correct. The law was not an attack on religious activity. It was designed to impose a work-free day of the week on the community. One is obliged to ask, however, whether such a goal truly represented a compelling state interest, whether it truly justified the limiting of religious freedom.

Regardless of Warren's adjudication in this case, he did make a broader point. He added that laws that placed an indirect burden on religious freedoms would lose their validity if the "state may accomplish its purpose by means which do not impose such a burden." In other words, if there was another way out of the problem—one that did not trample (even indirectly) on religious freedom—it should take priority. This didn't apply, by Warren's logic, in this particular case, but it remained an important principle.

This idea would gain much support in the years ahead, as would another staple of First Amendment jurisprudence: the idea of a compelling state interest. In some circumstances, the state was entitled to limit religious freedom. But how were such circumstances to be determined? Broadly put, the compelling state interest argument demanded that a tangible, urgent threat to social cohesion—as opposed to a minor inconvenience—be in evidence.

This idea came into focus during the 1963 case of *Sherbert v. Verner.* Adell Sherbert of South Carolina had been refused unemployment benefit on the grounds that she had failed to take on "suitable" work when it was offered. Religious freedom had been at the heart of her actions. Sherbert had worked at the same company for more than 30 years, but then a new policy was introduced requiring employees to work on Saturdays. As a Seventh-Day Adventist, for whom Saturday was the Sabbath, this was unacceptable to Sherbert, and after refusing to punch in on a Saturday, she lost her job. Moreover, a local state court and the South Carolina Supreme Court had decided that because Sherbert had willingly entered the ranks of the unemployed even though a job was still available to her, she did not deserve state benefits.

With a 7–2 majority the Supreme Court ruled that it was unconstitutional for the state to withhold unemployment benefit from an individual who turned down work because of her religious scruples. The law (which sensibly withheld benefits from those who had the option of a job) was deemed to be entirely valid, but the Court insisted that Sherbert was entitled to an exception from it. In a phrase with a long future ahead of it, Justice William Brennan argued that the state had not shown a "compelling state interest" for withholding benefits in this case. Essentially, what deep and irrevocable harm would have been done to South Carolina if it had reacted to exceptional circumstances in an exceptional way? Allowing Sherbert a pass because of her deeply held religious beliefs was unlikely to lead to a rash of indigent citizens abusing the state's welfare system. Only those with similar religious scruples would be able to claim precedent.

A similar line of reasoning applied in the 1972 case of *Wisconsin v. Yoder.* Laws in Wisconsin demanded the compulsory attendance of children at school until the age of 16. Unimpressed, Jonas Yoder stopped sending his children to school beyond the eighth grade on the grounds that (as an article of his Amish faith) it was against his religious beliefs to send his children to high school. The state countered with the argument that, religious beliefs of parents notwithstanding, it had a duty to offer the benefits of education to all the children under its care. The Supreme Court turned again to the notion of a "compelling state interest" and argued that the law for compulsory attendance infringed Yoder's right to free exercise. Once more, an exemption to an otherwise legitimate law was called for.

***

The pendulum seemed to be swinging toward expansive religious freedom, but as the 1980s and early 1990s demonstrated, it could sometimes move in the opposite direction. Again, the issue of when and where the state was entitled to limit freedoms was the central issue. The year 1983 witnessed the case of *Bob Jones University v. United States.* Bob Jones University in South Carolina described itself as a college that placed special emphasis on Christianity and the ethical content of Scripture. In 1971 the college had begun to allow African American students to enroll, but it continued to refuse admission to those involved in (or known to approve of) interracial marriage.

The IRS was far from being pleased with this development. On its books there was a policy whereby any private school that engaged in racial discrimination was to be stripped of its tax-exempt status. The university claimed that this was an assault on its religious freedom: the Bible, it argued, was the source of its position on interracial relationships. With a strong 8–1 majority, the Supreme Court backed the IRS's decision. It is hard to argue with this adjudication. If there was ever a compelling state interest, it resided in the effort to combat overt racism.

Few commentators, even many of the staunchest advocates of wide religious freedom, balked at the decision. Five years later, a more controversial case, *Lyng v. Northwest Indian Cemetery Protective Association,* entered the news cycle. Here, we require a slight digression into the role of Native American religion in America's debate about religious freedom and Church–State relations. After that, we'll get back on track and follow the Supreme Court's encounter with religious freedom cases over the last couple of decades.

## NATIVE AMERICAN RELIGION

From the earliest colonial days, Europeans justified their intrusions into the lands of indigenous peoples by appealing to an evangelical imperative. Spreading the Gospel was seen as one of the foremost duties of settlers in the New World, and such religious orders as the Jesuits and such dynamic individuals as John Eliot made huge efforts to win converts. Some of these missionaries were amiably curious about the religious environment in which they found themselves; others were dismissive of what they encountered. Almost without exception, they demanded change. This was the tenor of the times.

The arrival of the American Revolution did little to change this outlook, and throughout the 19th century, the protections of the First Amendment did not seem to extend to the ancient beliefs and practices of the nation's Indian tribes. So far as Church–State separation was concerned, it is crucial to note that the constant attempts to eradicate those beliefs and practices were routinely sponsored by government.

The Civilization Fund Act of 1819 summed up this approach. Federal money was to be used to support educators and missionaries charged with preventing "the further decline and final extinction of the Indian tribes, adjoining the frontier settlements of the United States, and for introducing among them the habits and arts of civilization the native peoples of the western territories." The dubious goal was that their "minds [would] become enlightened and expand, the Bible will be their book and they will grow up in habits of morality and industry." Throughout the 19th century, there was heated debate about how to confront the many Indian tribes. Some argued for a process of assimilation; others thought it best to isolate them on reservations. In both cases there was a basic assumption that the Indians' existing belief systems were abhorrent, and the century witnessed countless examples of forced relocation and what can only be described as cultural bullying.

Some political leaders and educators developed a pessimistic view. As Andrew Jackson explained in 1835, "all preceding experiments for the improvement of the Indians have failed. It seems now to be an established fact that they cannot live in contact with a civilized community and prosper. Ages of fruitless endeavours have at length brought us to a knowledge of this principle of intercommunication with them." Others remained convinced that the Indians could still be "civilized," and by the end of the century, there were hundreds of publicly funded educational institutions dedicated to eradicating all traces of Indian heritage from their pupils: names were changed, native languages were forbidden, and hair was cut, and needless to say, Christian instruction formed the heart of the syllabus.

Three planks of Indian policy were especially egregious. First, there was the determination to rob Indian tribes of any meaningful sense of initiative or self-governance: the Dawes Act of 1887, for instance, sought to put an end to communal land ownership. Second, there was a ferocious assault on tribal religion. Whenever native devotions began to enjoy a resurgence, they were attacked, sometimes brutally. So it was that the rapid spread of the so-called ghost dance in the 1880s culminated in the infamous slaughter at Wounded Knee. Finally, Indian holy places were routinely seized. In 1906, for example, a presidential order robbed the Pueblo of 48,000 acres (lands that included their most sacred sites), and in short measure, they were re-designated as part of Carson National Forest. They would not be returned until 1970.

During the first decades of the 20th century, some Americans began to query such policies and to argue that the First Amendment's ideals ought to apply to the nation's oldest communities. A degree of residual paternalism was often visible in these efforts, but men such as John Collier fought long, hard campaigns to extend religious freedom to Native American beliefs. As one of the masterminds behind the American Indian Defence Association (founded in 1923) and as Commissioner for Indian Affairs under Franklin Roosevelt, Collier aspired to an admirable goal: as he once put it, "no interference with Indian religious life or ceremonial expression will hereafter be tolerated . . . and fullest constitutional liberty in all matters affecting religion, conscience, and culture is insisted on for all Indians."

Collier did manage to win some notable victories, perhaps most notably the 1934 Indian Reorganization Act, which, though not universally popular among Native Americans, at least ended the policy of land allotment and returned a measure of self-rule to Indian communities. Specific legislative protection of Native American religious freedom was slower to arrive. It took until 1978 to pass the American Indian Religious Freedom Act, but when it finally arrived, it looked very straightforward: there was now a duty to "protect and preserve for American Indians their inherent right of freedom to believe, express and exercise the traditional religions of the American Indian."

As things turned out, interpreting this law was fraught with difficulties. First, for all the high rhetoric, the religious practices of Native Americans were sometimes still treated as a case apart. Struggles about the religious rights of Indians (perhaps most conspicuously the rights of Indian prisoners) continued to simmer. Second, the rights belatedly extended to Native Americans still had to confront the standards and strictures of First Amendment jurisprudence. Such rights, just like everyone else's, had to be balanced against the state's desire to sustain common order and social coherence. Enter, once again, the Supreme Court.

Old wounds were opened up by the 1988 case of *Lyng v. Northwest Indian Cemetery Protective Association.* The Chimney Rock area of the Six Rivers National Forest in California had been used over many generations by various American Indian tribes for their religious rituals. In 1982 the state's Forest Service established a study to determine the impact of building a road through the area. The study determined that plans for the road should be abandoned because it would possibly damage the areas used by the American Indians for their devotional purposes.

This suggestion was rejected by the Forest Service, and it drew up plans for a road that would stay as far away as possible from religious sites and areas of archaeological interest. Simultaneously, the Forest Service adopted a plan to allow the harvesting of timber in the area, though with the provision that religious sites would, again, be protected. A group representing the several Indian groups argued that this plan was likely to impact negatively on their right to free exercise of religion. The Supreme Court ruled that both of the Forest Services plans—the road and the timber-harvesting—were constitutional.

Two years later, a perhaps even more sensitive issue arrived on the Court's docket: *Employment Division, Department of Human Resources of Oregon v. Smith.* It turned out to be a crucially important case. A member of the Native American Church, Alfred Smith, had been fired from his job with a drug rehabilitation organization because of his sacramental use of the hallucinogen peyote. It was suggested that a user of one kind of drug was not the ideal employee for an institution charged with freeing others of their addictions. Consequently, Smith was denied unemployment benefits because he had been fired as a result of "misconduct."

In response, Smith claimed that this represented an infringement of his right to free exercise—partaking of peyote was part and parcel of his faith. The Supreme Court's majority decision, written by Justice Antonin Scalia, argued that a person's religious beliefs did not exempt him from a valid law that forbade behavior that the state is competent to regulate.

This was a momentous turning point because, in essence, the ruling rejected the notion that a "compelling state interest" had to be demonstrated before an infringement of religious liberty could be countenanced. Returning to an older standard, it was argued that a neutral, generally applicable law held sway over everyone's behavior, regardless of what effect it might have on an individual's ability to practice his religion.

## RELIGIOUS FREEDOM II

The Smith decision caused uproar. To some commentators, it seemed to demolish a legal standard, the compelling state interest, that for many years had done a decent job of squaring the circle between a right to free exercise and the government's need to reign in religiously motivated behavior that threatened social and political order. Congress acted quickly, and in 1993 it passed the Religious Freedom Restoration Act (RFRA), intended to restore the concept of the "compelling state interest." There had to be good and urgent reason for the state to trample on religious freedoms.

The response was swift, in Supreme Court terms. In the epochal 1997 case of *City of Boerne v. Flores,* the constitutionality of the RFRA was challenged. The Archbishop of San Antonio had applied for a permit to make extensions to a church in Boerne, Texas. The application was denied on the basis of an existing statute intended to preserve historical areas in the city. The archbishop took his case to the district court on the grounds that the denial of the permit had been a breach of the recently enshrined RFRA. The City of Boerne argued, contrariwise, that the RFRA was itself unconstitutional because it overrode existing local preservation ordinances. By the time the case reached the Supreme Court, a basic idea had come into focus. Had Congress exceeded the powers granted by the Fourteenth Amendment by enacting the RFRA? The court's answer, by 6–2, was yes, given these particular circumstances, it had.

Nothing is ever straightforward in the realm of free exercise jurisprudence, however, and recent years have seen various decisions and legislative moves that seem to shore up a belief in expansive religious freedom. One such instance was the cumbersomely named 2000 Religious Land Use and Institutionalized Persons Act (RLUIPA), a federal law that, among other things, prohibited government from limiting prisoners' religious freedom without first showing a compelling reason for so doing. This came under scrutiny in the 2005 case of *Cutter v. Wilkinson,* which challenged the act by virtue of its government-sponsored advancement of prisoners' religious beliefs. This, it was said, actually breached the establishment clause (here we gain a sense of how convoluted these arguments can become). In this instance, the Supreme Court determined that the federal law, intended to protect religious freedoms, was perfectly acceptable.

Similarly, in the 2005 case of *Gonzales v. O Centro Espirita Beneficiente Uniao Do Vegetal* (UDV), another notable victory was scored for the exercise of religious freedom. UDV, as a religious organization, disliked governmental interference that questioned its right to use hoasca during its religious ceremonies. Hoasca was a prohibited drug according to the Controlled Substances Act, but once more referring to the RFRA, the UDV argued that it was entitled to express its religious sensibilities as it saw fit.

A local district court agreed, as did the 10th Circuit Court of Appeals. The issue before the Supreme Court was whether the RFRA demanded that the government allow the use of an otherwise illegal drug by a religious organization, even when Congress had determined that such a drug was open to abuse in other circumstances. By a startling 8–0 majority, the Court agreed with the proposition. There was no "compelling reason" to prevent the UDV from using the drug in the limited circumstances of their religious observances.

## THE WALL OF SEPARATION

Making, enforcing, and adjusting laws that dealt with the exercise of religious freedom was always destined to be a tortuously difficult process, and the correct response to the contradictions and confusions of recent Supreme Court decisions is surely one of confusion mixed with heartfelt appreciation for the effort to negotiate such perilous legal terrain. At the core of the dilemma is the attempt to square the individual's right to free exercise and the state's duty to uphold good order. It would never be possible to fashion an ideal solution that pleased everyone concerned.

Perhaps cases dealing directly with Church–State interaction and entanglement would be a more straightforward undertaking. Sadly, this did not prove to be the case. For more than two hundred years, Americans have sought to abide by the First Amendment's ruling on Church–State separation. Unfortunately, and as we have already seen, it has always been hard to determine what that ruling actually stated or, just as importantly, what it implied beyond its specific prohibitions. Some matters became relatively uncontroversial. The notion of a nationally established faith, for example, was immediately abandoned during the early years of the Republic, and by the middle of the 19th century, there was no longer a state in the Union that financially supported a specific Christian denomination through general taxation.

All the First Amendment actually demands, however, is that "Congress shall make no law respecting an establishment of religion." This still leaves ample room for many controversial issues to be debated. Does the prohibition of an established Church necessarily lead to the conclusion that any direct entanglement between faith and politics is to be avoided? What is to be done when religious ideas enter political discourse or when religious symbols appear in public buildings or on public property?

Those who argue for an especially strict separation between Church and State often insist that any blatant intermingling of political and religious concerns is unconstitutional. They point to any number of infringements: the fact that, since 1954, the Pledge of Allegiance has included the phrase "under God"; that the phrase "In God We Trust" is still on the currency circulated by federal mints; that the highest public official in the land, the President, routinely ends his addresses with the words "God Bless America"; that legislatures still have their chaplains; and that America has a National Day of Prayer. Even in the Supreme Court, the very place where the issue of Church and State is codified, the court marshal's proclamation at the opening of every session ends with "God save the United States and this honorable court."

Other commentators adopt a more indulgent approach to such phenomena. They argue that it would be foolish to deny the religious roots of America's laws and cultural assumptions or to overlook the fact that many Americans are still people of faith. They suggest that enforcing the very specific rubrics of the First Amendment does not necessitate the casting out of religion from all public discourse. More than that, they fear that the attempts to achieve such a goal would leave America bereft: the moral compass and important legacy provided by America's religious past would be lost, and we would be left, in the famous phrase, with a naked public square in which religious voices would no longer be heard.

Some people in this latter camp often argue that the more zealous Church–State separationists are not really following the letter of the First Amendment at all. In fact, it is alleged, they are in thrall to the Jeffersonian metaphor of a strict wall of separation: a powerful image but one that, because it only appeared in a letter from Jefferson to the Baptists of Danbury, enjoys absolutely no constitutional authority. The whole notion of Church–State separation, some would suggest, is the result of historical happenstance and the accretion of post-constitutional politicking.

It is, to say the very least, a heated debate and one that shows few signs of disappearing. Over the past 60 years, the Supreme Court has been charged with negotiating this awkward terrain.

\*\*\*

The major turning point came in 1947 with the case of *Everson v. Board of Education of Ewing Township.* This was the first time the Supreme Court applied the establishment clause to a state, New Jersey, by means of the Fourteenth Amendment. What would happen when a state law seemed to breach federally mandated dictums? The issue at hand was whether it was appropriate to use state funds to pay for buses that took students to private schools—many of which had transparent religious affiliations. One resident of Ewing Township, Arch Everson, believed that this practice, as sanctioned by a 1941 statute, represented a flagrant breach of the First Amendment. Everson averred that the state, by shelling out for the buses, was actively aiding avowedly religious institutions.

The court, in a very close ruling (5–4), disagreed and argued that the provision of state funds for the purpose of busing children to school did not violate the First Amendment. It all came down to who the direct beneficiary of the state funds happened to be: the child, who certainly deserved to receive an education, or the school to which he or she was being sent. The *Everson* majority decision echoed an earlier case from 1930, *Cochran v. Louisiana Board of Education,* in which the court sanctioned a Louisiana law that allowed public funds to be spent on the provision of textbooks (dealing exclusively with nonreligious topics) for students in parochial schools.

The notion here was that providing such books (much like providing transport) was primarily to the advantage of the individual children, not the institutions they attended. This came to be known as the child-benefit theory.

The *Everson* case hinted at another rubric that would continue to be debated over the coming decades. It was crucial for government to maintain a *neutral* attitude when dealing with religion and religious institutions (almost everyone agreed that this was the obvious implication of the First Amendment), but there was a danger that attempting to uphold this neutrality could cross over into an adversarial or hostile approach—not treating such institutions in an equitable way.

As Justice Hugo Black explained, in a soaring but still controversial phrase, there ought to be "a high and impregnable wall of separation between Church and State." The difficulty resided in determining the bricks and mortar of which that wall was constructed. Each decision—and this was surely the thing that the Supreme Court got exactly right—had to be judged on its individual merits. If something happened that seemed to offend the terms of the First Amendment, a series of important questions always had to be asked. What was the law in question intended to achieve (obvious support of a religious institution or the upholding of privileges and opportunities that every American citizen ought to enjoy)? Was the law an example of avoidable entanglement between Church and State, or did it serve a legitimate purpose that was of benefit to the intended recipients rather than a specific religious institution?

And perhaps most importantly of all (and here we return to the issue discussed previously), was the First Amendment designed to banish religion from the public sphere or simply to prohibit extreme examples of political and religious cross-pollination—occasions when it was abundantly clear that public funds and support were benefiting a specific religious denomination?

Answering such questions proved to be very difficult, and the decades after *Everson* saw many cases coming before the Supreme Court. It would be fair to say that the Court has exhibited a schizophrenic attitude when dealing with such matters, although this can perhaps be explained by nothing more complicated than the shifting attitudes of the jurists who have sat on its benches. Some Supreme Court justices have been rigorists, whereas others have been more flexible, and the cynic might suggest that the Court's decisions have been something of a crap-game: decisions have only ever really depended on which of these groups is in the majority. This, after all, is why the election of a new member of the Court still sends various partisan groups into apoplexies of activity: they know, full well, that it as all about the math.

The other certainty is that, in the realm of Church–State jurisprudence, the relationship between religion and education will continue to be the most contested and most often revisited arena. It wasn't long after *Everson* that this started to become abundantly clear.

*** 

The year 1948 witnessed the case of *McCollum v. Board of Education.* It was decided that allowing religious groups to use classrooms in Illinois public schools to teach religious ideas represented a breach of the First Amendment. Whatever ones druthers, this has all the hallmarks of a fairly straightforward decision. First, the religious groups went about their business during ordinary school hours (so the extracurricular argument immediately fell down). Second, the meetings were patently of immediate benefit to the religious groups concerned. They allowed them to preach their message, and from a child-benefit point of view, missing such meetings would not have disadvantaged the participants in terms of their acquisition of a rounded education. Stopping such meetings simply wasn't the same as preventing a child from being bused to school (as in *Everson*) or from reading secular textbooks (as in *Cochran*). Crucially, it all took place in the classrooms of publicly funded schools.

What, though, if similarly religiously motivated activities took place elsewhere? This was the question posed by *Zorach v. Clauson* in 1952. A program in New York allowed students in public schools time off from their timetabled classes in order to partake of religious instruction. These classes were mounted during regular school hours, but crucially, they were not carried out on public school grounds. It was an entirely voluntary scheme, and if parents chose to avail themselves of it, they could claim that they were simply sending their children to religious classes that matched their faith—an opportunity that, by the very terms of the First Amendment, was not available to them in the public classroom. These were very muddy waters, but Tessim Zorach insisted that the scheme was unconstitutional.

In a 6–3 decision, the Supreme Court decided that Zorach was wrong. It held that there was a substantial difference between religious programs that took place on school property (as had been the case in *McCollum*) and those that did not (as in *Zorach*). This was a reasonable adjudication, but the justices involved clearly sensed that bigger issues were in play.

Once again, a legal concept with a bright future was articulated. Building on the idea of avoiding hostility (as opposed to sustaining neutrality) in Church–State matters, Justice William O. Douglas argued for a need to "accommodate" the desires and aspirations of a "religious people whose institutions presuppose a Supreme Being." There is endless room to debate the notion that Americans are, in fact, such a people (many Americans, then as now, would disagree with the basic premise), but so far as Douglas was concerned, the program in New York was not relying on the public purse; it took place away from public school grounds; and ultimately, it simply allowed those of religious beliefs to send their children for religious instruction. He saw no reason why this represented an entanglement between Church and State, and although his rhetoric was probably unfortunate, his legal standpoint was perfectly reasonable.

Matters would become more complicated when the expression of religious belief took place on public grounds. This was the issue that McCollum had already confronted, and in 1962 it was revisited in *Engel v. Vitale*.

New York was once again the setting. The State Board of Regents had composed a prayer, and it recommended that it be read aloud in the public schools of the New York school system. The religious nature of the prayer was unambiguous. "Almighty God, we acknowledge our dependence upon Thee, and we beg Thy blessings upon us, our parents, our teachers and our Country." This was quite obviously religion entering the public school, and unsurprisingly, some parents were deeply unhappy with the initiative. Ten of them, including Steven Engel, and backed by the ACLU, insisted that making their children recite or listen to such a prayer was a blatant breach of the establishment clause. With a healthy 6–1 majority, the Supreme Court concurred.

The prayer was adjudged to be an obvious religious activity, and it was asserted that government, or one of its branches (the Board of Regents in this case), had no business composing prayers for public schools. There was a suggestion that the voluntary nature of the prayer ought to be considered—no child was literally forced to mouth along—but the Court's majority ruling dismissed this idea because of the coercive pressure to conform faced by children in the classroom.

The *Engel* decision was met with an astonishing public response. It became the stuff of countless op-ed pieces, newspaper cartoons, and sometimes combative debate. At this point, more seemed to be at stake than the interpretation of the law. Many groups, notably those of Jewish and Baptist affiliation, were delighted with the decision. Others were less pleased. Francis Cardinal Spellman said that he was both "shocked and frightened . . . that a Supreme Court has declared unconstitutional a simple and voluntary declaration of belief in God by public school children." The era's leading Protestant evangelist, Billy Graham, was even blunter: "God pity our country," he announced.

Erwin Griswold, then dean of Harvard Law School, revealed his opinions in a speech in Utah:

This is a country of religious toleration. That is a great consequence of our history embodied in the First Amendment. But does religious toleration mean a religious sterility? . . . This, I venture to say again, has been, and is, a Christian country, in origin, history, tradition and culture. It was out of Christian doctrine and ethics, I think it can be said, that it developed its notion of toleration . . . But does the fact that we have officially adopted toleration as our standard mean that we must give up our history and our tradition?

Many agreed with Griswold's logic, and the years after the *Engel* decision witnessed the proposal of dozens of constitutional amendments (that of Frank Becker of New York is the most famous) that would have made a protected right out of prayer and biblical reading. None of them were destined to pass.

It is very difficult to cut through the hysteria and partisanship that surrounded the Engel affair. From a legal perspective, the decision was probably in tune with the prevailing trajectory of Supreme Court decisions. Those of separatist sympathies (and even those of moderate accomodationist views) found little that was exceptionable. It was at this point, however, that mass opinion truly entered the debate about Church and State.

Rightly or wrongly, some Americans began to insist that the sensible rubrics of the First Amendment were being taken to an unfortunate extreme. The baby, so to speak, was being thrown out with the bathwater. The result was one of America's routine culture wars.

Those who had been infuriated by *Engel* were certainly not soothed by the subsequent 1963 case of *School District of Abington Township v. Schempp*. Entering very similar territory to the Engel decision, this case concerned a Pennsylvania statute that enforced a daily reading from the Bible in the state's public schools. The law also insisted that students could be excused from such readings upon the written request of their parents. Far from seeing this as a convenient get-out clause, however, some parents argued that their consciences, and those of their children, were being assaulted.

Roger and Donna Schempp attended one of the Philadelphia schools where these biblical verses were recited over the intercom at the start of the day and were followed by a reading of the Lord's Prayer. The Schempp children's parents (both Unitarians), instead of having their children excused from these exercises (which they feared would damage the children's relationship with students and faculty), challenged the constitutionality of the statute on the grounds that such Bible readings violated the establishment clause.

In an 8–1 ruling, which clearly backed up the *Engel* adjudication, the Supreme Court agreed that such an exclusive religious exercise in the public schools clearly failed to meet the standard of neutrality in the state's relationship with religion. A specific religious message was being broadcasted in a public school. Justice Tom Clark, writing for the majority, also posited an important test by which such statutes ought to be measured against the establishment clause in future: in order to be deemed constitutional, a law would have to aim at a valid secular purpose, and it should neither hinder nor advance religion. On this basis, the law under discussion in Schempp was held to be inappropriate.

\*\*\*

Some commentators found this brace of decisions unpalatable. It was suggested that some justices had been unhelpfully doctrinaire. In the Everson case, for instance, Justice Jackson had had this to say: "This freedom was first in the Bill of Rights because it was first in the forefathers' minds; it was set forth in absolute terms, and its strength is its rigidity. It was intended not only to keep the state's hands out of religion but to keep religion's hands off the state and, above all, to keep bitter religious controversy out of public life by denying to every denomination an advantage from getting control of public policy or the public purse."

Some queried the consequences of this statement and suggested that the notion of rigidity was illegitimate. Was this really what the First Amendment had intended, or was this perhaps more to do with the Jeffersonian notion of a wall of separation that had no constitutional sanction? As one justice would argue, "a rule of law should not be drawn from a figure of speech." Some jurists and legal scholars continue to plow this interpretative acre.

In the immediate wake of these early 1960s Church–State cases, it is possible to discern a hostile response within some sectors of the American public. Whether this represented majority opinion is much harder to calculate, not least because the gainsayers were much more vocal. What can be stated with certainty is that the *Engel* decision changed American politics forever. It was one of the triggers for the emergence of the Christian Right, which, during the subsequent few decades, would make considerable political hay out of its campaign to return America to its Christian roots and to prevent (by its reckoning) the excessive secularization of American culture.

The Supreme Court also caught scent of the negative response to *Engel,* and in various subsequent decisions, it sought to rein in what it perceived as an excessively separationist outlook. Acommodationism became the buzz word.

In 1968 the Court dealt with *Board of Education of Central School District No. 1 v. Allen.* A program in New York allowed state-approved texts to be lent, free of charge, to students in grades 7 through 12 in both private and parochial schools. It was argued, first, that only secular books were involved, so the state was living up to the standard of neutrality and, second, that the program was intended to benefit the children involved and not the institutions they attended. The old child-benefit theory.

Members of one New York school board were not so sure, and they regarded the program as a violation of the establishment clause. Books, paid for through public taxation, were being given to religious schools. The trouble was, members of the school board in question feared that if they did not comply with the program, they would face dismissal by the commissioner of education, James E. Allen Jr. Confronted with this dilemma, they chose to challenge the constitutionality of the law. The Supreme Court ruled that the New York program was, in fact, constitutional—it had a "secular legislative purpose and a primary effect that neither advances nor inhibits religion." Only the children would reap the benefits.

Two years later, another victory for a less stringent approach to Church–State separation was secured in *Walz v. Tax Commission of the City of New York.* The New York City Tax Commission had routinely granted tax exemptions to religious, charitable, and educational nonprofit groups. Frederick Walz argued that, so far as religious organizations were concerned, this breached the establishment clause and that property owners who were not eligible for such exemptions were indirectly making contributions to religious groups. In a decision that continued the Court's accommodationist trend, Warren Burger upheld the constitutionality of the exemption.

Matters were becoming increasingly confused, but the Supreme Court has always been in thrall to the notion of an acid test for controversial legal issues. It makes life easier. Such a test arrived in 1971 with the case of *Lemon v. Kurtzman.* This case centered on the constitutionality of statutes in Pennsylvania and Rhode Island. Since 1968, legislation had been operative in Pennsylvania whereby public funds could be used to reimburse private schools (religious ones included) to pay for textbooks, salaries, and other materials. It was made clear, however, that all books and materials had to be approved by the Superintendent of Public Instruction, and teachers were only to be reimbursed when they had been teaching *secular* subjects. There was no direct, state-supported religious instruction, and the children affected were the direct beneficiaries. One Pennsylvania teacher, Alton Lemon, claimed that the statute violated the establishment clause of the First Amendment by using public funds to support religious institutions.

In Rhode Island, a similar 1969 statute had allowed public funds to be used to enhance the salaries of teachers in private schools (many of which, in Rhode Island, were Catholic-run) for the teaching of secular subjects. This time around, both laws were deemed unconstitutional by the Supreme Court. Warren Burger, who had ruled in a seemingly opposite direction in *Walz,* once more turned to the notion of excessive entanglement and argued that, in this instance, the statutes were benefiting the institutions themselves rather than the students and parents they served.

Famously, Burger offered a three-part test by which such cases ought to be judged in the future. To be regarded as constitutional, a law must have a secular purpose, it must have the effect of neither advancing nor inhibiting religion, and it must not produce excessive entanglement between government and religion. Burger believed passionately that he was being consistent.

The Lemon test, as it came to be known, had a certain elegance, but not unlike the First Amendment, it was long on generalities and short on specifics. Talking about a secular purpose, or about the goal of neither helping nor hindering religion, or about the perils of excessive entanglement was easy enough. Deciding what such terms and aspirations actually meant proved to be rather more difficult.

There was no issue more tricky than the one that had provoked all of this legal theorizing—the place of education in public schools. And new controversies emerged—most notably expressions of religious belief in the public domain, be it nativity crèches on public property or monuments celebrating the Ten Commandments in and around the nation's law courts and public buildings.

## SCHOOLS, AGAIN

By the mid-1980s, Americans had become accustomed to the issue of prayer in public schools eating up column inches in their newspapers and taking up an inordinate amount of shelf room in their local bookstores. It was also a vibrant issue for those involved in the political process. During his 1976 and 1980 presidential campaigns, Ronald Reagan had made the intro-duction of a prayer amendment one of the goals of his platform, and in 1984 he sponsored just such a measure. It stated that "nothing in this Constitution shall be construed to prohibit individual or group prayers in public schools or other public institutions." In March of that year, the proposed amendment won a vote in the Senate, though only by a margin of 56 to 44, short of the two-thirds majority required.

That Reagan supported such a measure came as no surprise. As early as 1982, he had complained at a national prayer breakfast that "God, the source of all knowledge, has been expelled from the classroom," but the Senate vote and the publicity that surrounded it demonstrated just how divided America was on the issue. There were to be endless tussles over school prayer in the years to come: the notion of a constitutional amendment did not disappear, and scholars and commentators argued endlessly about the differences be-tween voluntary and compulsory prayers, or between an explicit invocation of religious ideas and a simple moment of silence in public classrooms, dur-ing which students who were so-minded could offer up mental obeisances to their maker.

These last two issues came before the Supreme Court with the 1985 case of *Wallace v. Jaffree*. Ishmael Jaffree, a resident of Mobile County, Alabama, was an agnostic. His children attended a public school where, in accordance with a state statute, the day began with a moment of voluntary prayer. His children told him that although the prayer was discretionary, their failure to participate had damaged their relationship with their classmates. Jaffree therefore challenged the constitutionality of the Alabama statute, along with two earlier laws that had mandated moments of silence and meditation at the start of the school day. The Supreme Court found no fault with a statute that introduced a moment of silence in the public schools, but it decided that the addition of the call for voluntary prayer was unconstitutional.

Justice William Rehnquist, who was fast becoming the leading champion of more accommodationist attitudes, offered an important dissenting decision, however. He denounced the Jeffersonian idea of a wall of separation between

Church and State as being "based on bad history, a metaphor which has proved useless as a guide to judging." This resistance to erecting unnecessary barriers between religion and the public sphere would only grow in popularity over the coming decades.

At first blush, the 1992 case of *Lee v. Weisman* seemed to represent a notable victory for the separationists, but it was not quite so straightforward. When Merith Weisman graduated from Nathan Bishop Middle School, Providence, Rhode Island, a Baptist minister was employed to attend the ceremony and offer up an invocation of thanks to Christ for his role in the students' accomplishments. Merith's father, Daniel Weisman, a Jew, complained to the school. Despite this, three years later, when Weisman's younger daughter was due to graduate, an invocation and a benediction were once more planned for the ceremonies. The school's principal contacted a local rabbi to carry out these duties, but Weisman was still dissatisfied, and he sought restraining orders to prevent *any* cleric from delivering a prayer at the graduation.

The inclusion of a prayer was deemed unconstitutional by the U.S. Court of Appeals for the First Circuit, and with a 5–4 majority, the Supreme Court also deemed state-sponsored prayer at a public school's graduation ceremony to be a violation of the establishment clause. Whether or not the prayer was sectarian was adjudged irrelevant, and crucially, because attendance at the ceremony was compulsory, the prayer represented a variety of indirect coercion on the part of the school authorities.

It is important to stress, however, that it was the coercion that most infuriated the Court. The more basic issue of a wall of separation was questioned by many of the justices involved. Justice Kennedy averred that "a relentless and all-pervasive attempt to exclude religion from every aspect of public life could itself become inconsistent with the Constitution. We recognise that at graduation time and throughout the course of the educational process, there will be instances when religious values, religious practises and religious persons will have some interaction with the public schools and their students."

Moreover, as Justice Antonin Scalia explained in his dissenting opinion, it was a mistake to deny the fact that religion was part of American heritage and culture. The Court's decision in *Weisman,* he insisted, was "conspicuously bereft of any reference to history" and laid "waste a tradition that is as old as public school graduation ceremonies themselves." The argument from coercion, meanwhile, was a red herring. Through its convoluted "instrument of destruction, the bulldozer of its social engineering, the Court invents a boundless, and boundlessly manipulable, test of psychological coercion." Scalia's basic point was that religion had always played some role in public life because that is what the American people demanded. "Today's opinion shows more forcefully than tomes of argumentation why our nation's protection,

that fortress which is out constitution, cannot possibly rest upon the changeable philosophical predilections of the justices of this court, but must have
deep foundations in the historic practises of our people." By any standard,
and there is much room to query Scalia's argument, this was a bold analysis.

***

Religion in the schools had always been about more than prayer, of course,
and a similar to-and-fro between competing judicial factions can also be discerned in a host of other issues. The 1985 case of *Aguilar v. Felton* concerned
the sending of public school teachers and others (including guidance coun-
selors and psychologists) to religious schools in New York to provide remedial
instruction. Various safeguards were put in place to limit the teachers' involvement with religion while in the schools, but Betty-Louise Felton and other
New York residents claimed that the program still breached the establishment
clause of the First Amendment. Having journeyed through the lower courts,
the case came before the Supreme Court in 1985, and it was decided, with a
5–4 majority, that the program was unconstitutional.

The 5–4 ruling was a sign of a deeply divided court, and rather spectacu-
larly, this earlier decision was overturned just over a decade later by the ruling
in *Agostini v. Felton*. By the stroke of a judicial pen, sending public school
teachers to provide remedial education in private schools was now deemed
constitutional, and this was a logic already articulated in the 1993 case of
*Zobrest v. Catalina Foothills School District*. James Zobrest was enrolled at
the Salpointe Catholic High School in Tucson, Arizona. When his parents
asked the local school district to provide James with a sign language inter-
preter, their request was declined on the grounds that this would violate the
establishment clause of the First Amendment. In a 5–4 decision, the Supreme
Court held that the school district had acted wrongly, given that the beneficiary of the Zobrests' request (which was directed at a "neutral government
program": the provision of sign interpreters) would have been the child, not
the school he attended. A similar trend can also be discerned in the 2000 case
of *Mitchell v. Helms*, which allowed the provision of computer hardware and
software directly to primary and secondary parochial schools.

Because of such cases, there was a tangible sense of the Court moving toward a more accommodationist position. This, along with the provisions of
the 1984 Equal Access Act, was seized upon by many religious groups who
claimed a right to hold their meetings on public school property. The question had been raised in 1990 by *Westside Community Schools v. Mergens*. At
Westside High School in Omaha, Nebraska, students were allowed to participate in various groups and clubs that met on school premises after school
hours. Bridget Mergens sought to establish a Christian club as part of this

initiative, but on the grounds that, because all groups required a faculty sponsor, this risked violating the establishment clause, the school board denied her request. Invoking the Equal Access Act, Mergens claimed that this was unjust. Similar principles were at stake in the 1995 case of *Rosenberger v. The Rector and Visitors of the University of Virginia,* in which the Court denounced the university's policy of denying funds to an evangelical Christian student newspaper, not least because more than 100 other student publications and clubs were entitled to such funds.

Similar issues arose in *Good News Club v. Milford Central School.* For good reason this case has been identified as a watershed moment in the chipping away at a more rigorous separationist agenda. Two central, and conflicting, issues were at stake: first, whether (in the wider context of creating a limited public forum) denying a Christian group (the Good News Club) access to public school facilities represented a violation of its freedom of speech, and second, whether allowing access would be a violation of the establishment clause. The Supreme Court agreed to the first proposition but denied the second. It found that the public school in New York had violated the Good News Club's free speech rights when it denied it access to the after-school limited public forum. It also found that the school's concern about an establishment clause violation did not justify the limitation of the Club's right to free speech.

*** 

Reeling off such cases, though instructive, can easily lead to confusion, not least because when one decision goes the way of separation, another seems to point toward a more indulgent judicial attitude. Thus, only a year before the Good News Club decision, the Court heard *Santa Fe School District v. Doe.* This case asked whether a school district's policy of allowing student-led prayer at football games was constitutional. The Court ruled that the practice was a violation of the establishment clause. There was no doubt that the speech in question was attributable to the state: it was delivered at a school-sponsored event, over the school's public address system, and by an individual who was seen as representing the student body. There was also an issue of coercion, given that some students were faced with the choice of missing the games or exposing themselves to religious practice that they and their parents found objectionable.

Things do seem to be in constant flux, and reaching any robust conclusion about how the Supreme Court will respond to cases that deal with religion in the public schools over the next few years is very difficult. It seems likely that a more accommodationist attitude and a reluctance to rely too heavily on the old Jeffersonian metaphor of a wall of separation will be with us for some time. We are also probably going to see many more adjudications in which there is talk of the cultural legacy of America's Christian past and the continuing religious identity of many of its people.

Whether this is a reflection of reality or a retrograde step depends very much on whom you ask. The prospect delights some commentators and fills others with horror. Objectively speaking, it seems sensible to interrogate, as closely as possible, existing judicial assumptions about what the First Amendment implies in the realm of Church–State relations. There is something positive in the fact that members of the highest court in the nation are deeply embroiled in answering questions that concern all Americans: Does the prohibition of a religious establishment necessarily lead to a substantial separation between religion and public life? How loyal should we be to the intentions of the nation's founding fathers, assuming that such intentions are either consistent or easily discernible?

The devil is in the detail: in the differences, for instance, between coerced prayer and voluntary prayer, between sectarian and nonsectarian prayer, between religious groups meeting during the school day and after-hours, and—perhaps most importantly of all—between moments of Church–State entanglement that are advantageous to the child and those that are of most benefit to the religious institution.

One thing is clear: the decisions that are made will depend largely on who is making them. Scalia's insistence that interpretation of the Constitution "cannot possibly rest upon the changeable philosophical predilections of the justices of this court" is, frankly, pie-in-the-sky and perhaps a little rich coming from a forceful, agenda-rich justice such as Scalia. In fact, the interpretation of the Constitution will always be hugely influenced by the philosophical druthers of the nine justices who sit on the Washington bench. The result is incoherence and mutability, but it is hard to identify a preferable alternative.

## TEN COMMANDMENTS AND NINE PUZZLED JURISTS

The whirligig of legal decisions that have confronted the issue of religion in the public schools has often been calmed by a single, simple idea. If it could be shown that the fruits of entanglement between Church and State (which usually meant the deployment of public funds, materials, or personnel) were mainly aimed at improving the life and prospects of a child, then there was room for maneuver. Strict separationists have often balked at this idea, but even if it is legally questionable (and that is a source of much debate), it at least has the virtue of compassion and common sense. Why should children be disadvantaged because their parents can't quite decide how to curate the First Amendment? As emotive arguments go, this one has proved very popular.

In the grown-up world, such an alternative is not readily available. The past few decades have seen an explosion of Church–State arguments in realms far beyond the school classroom. America, from state to state and from county to county, is a patchwork of public spaces—those areas and arenas, from courtrooms to parks, that not only are paid for through public taxation but that also strive to encapsulate America's civic identity. What happens when religion enters such territory? Is this a reflection of the will of the American majority and an homage to America's religious past and present, or is it a flagrant violation of Church–State separation? As you might be able to guess by now, the jury is still out, although, if recent Supreme Court decisions are anything to go by, it seems to be leaning more in one direction than the other.

Let's start with something as innocent-sounding as a Christmas nativity scene and then end with one of the most controversial (and most reported) Church–State issues of recent times—displays of the Ten Commandments.

***

Throughout the 20th century, it was far from uncommon to see Christmas displays on public American property. It was a seasonal expectation in many towns and cities, but did that make it constitutional? This was the question probed by the 1984 case of *Lynch v. Donnelly.* The city of Pawtucket, Rhode Island, maintained a Christmas display that included a nativity scene alongside other, nonreligious items, including a Christmas tree, wishing wells, and a Santa Claus house. The Court had to decide whether such a display, placed on public land, violated the establishment clause. With a 5–4 majority, the Court ruled that it did not, and great emphasis was placed on the fact that other nonreligious items were included in the display. It was argued that although the nativity scene undoubtedly had a religious message, the display as a whole aimed at a secular purpose by demonstrating the origins of a national public holiday. Justice Warren Burger rooted his decision on a rejection of an absolutist reading of the establishment clause and the fact that there was "an unbroken history of official acknowledgment by all three branches of government of the role of religion in American life from at least 1789."

Some found this adjudication shaky, or perhaps more accurately, they found Burger's talk of unbroken religious traditions less than helpful. Once again, a Supreme Court justice had backed up his perfectly reasonable legal adjudication with divisive rhetoric. Perhaps the fact that the decision was made in the middle of the 1980s, when such rhetoric was very much in vogue, goes a long way toward explaining this.

The 1989 case of *County of Allegheny v. ACLU* helped to clarify matters. Everything seemed to depend on the nature of the displays in question: on whether they included obviously religious paraphernalia and, crucially, on whether such paraphernalia represented the beliefs of one religious tradition to the exclusion of all others. In Pittsburgh, Pennsylvania, a nativity scene (donated by a local Catholic organization and quite obviously a celebration of Christian beliefs) had been erected in the Allegheny County courthouse. No other religious displays accompanied it. Outside the city-county building, there was another display that included a menorah (owned by a Jewish organization) and a large Christmas tree.

The Supreme Court made a sharp, and probably quite sensible, distinction between the two. It ruled that the nativity scene was unconstitutional because it "sends an unmistakeable message that it supports and promotes the Christian praise of God" but that the display including the menorah was acceptable within the terms of the establishment clause. It simply recognized, in a non-exclusivist way, that Christmas and Hanukah were a familiar part of the nation's winter holiday season.

It could be argued that Americans get unnecessarily hot under the collar when it comes to Christmas displays. After all, there are easy alternatives available. You could simply erect such displays through private initiatives and away from public grounds. Literally a few feet would make all the difference in terms of the establishment clause. An issue such as religion in public schools is very difficult to resolve (there are a dozen scenarios that require serious meditation); the consequences of nativity scenes and their ilk are much easier to iron out. Fighting on principle, when the battle could easily be avoided, seems bizarre.

But such conflicts have not been limited to the Christmas season. As lawyers and repeat-offenders know, many American courtrooms and courthouses are home to religious imagery. Short of whitewashing the walls, there is little that can be done about this. But the introduction of a new religiously minded statue, plaque, or monument on public land or in public buildings can be a very different matter.

***

In 1980 the Supreme Court dealt with the case of *Stone v. Graham*. A Kentucky law, dating from 1978, required a copy of the Ten Commandments to be displayed in every public school classroom. These posters were careful to include a note that there was no religious intent behind their display but that the Ten Commandments represented an integral part of the legal tradition of the nation. The Supreme Court, overturning earlier decisions in lower courts, argued that the law was unconstitutional. It had no secular purpose, and its main aim was of a religious nature. The establishment clause had been breached.

So much for classrooms, but what about courtrooms and other public buildings? It was not uncommon to hear the argument that the Ten Commandments had played an important role in shaping America's legal ideals, so perhaps it was entirely fitting to display them in public arenas. In February 2002, the Supreme Court declined to become embroiled in this sensitive issue and refused to hear the case of *O'Bannon v. Indiana Civil Liberties Union*. The ICLU had jumped into action after the state's governor, Frank O'Bannon, had allowed a seven-foot-tall Ten Commandments monument to take up residence on the statehouse lawn in Indianapolis. The U.S. Seventh Circuit Court of Appeals determined that the monument violated Church–State separation, and by refusing to hear an appeal, the Supreme Court allowed this ruling to stand. The argument was not over, however.

Roy Moore was a state supreme court justice in Alabama. He had long demonstrated a penchant for displays of the Ten Commandments, displaying them in his courtroom while a state judge. In the summer of 2001, he decided to erect a two-ton, four-foot-tall monument of the Commandments in the state judicial building in Montgomery.

Unsurprisingly, the move caused uproar. Acting for various local residents, the ACLU, Americans United for Separation of Church and State, and the Southern Poverty Law Center filed suit against Moore. In November 2002 a local district court ruled that the monument breached the separation of Church and State: it was, so the ruling argued, an obtrusive, year-round display with obvious religious intent.

Moore appealed, but in July 2003, the 11th U.S. Circuit Court concurred with the earlier decision. It rejected Moore's argument from tradition and his suggestion that, in his capacity as a senior state justice, he was exempt from obeying federal rules was thrown out of court.

Moore refused to remove the monument, and as a result, he was suspended from his legal duties. A veritable media circus unfolded, and the local community was deeply divided. The monument was finally removed but only in the face of public protests, organized by local religious groups, that required the interventions of state police officers.

Moore attempted to take his cause to the Supreme Court, but the Court refused to get involved. The response to this curious incident was quite extraordinary. Some Alabama politicians even went to the extreme of proposing a Ten Commandments Defense Act, and at one stage, the House of Representatives had added an amendment to an appropriations bill, aimed at preventing the enforcement of the circuit court's order to remove the monument.

Rhetorical temperatures were high, and in the coming months and years, controversies involving Commandment displays (notably in Frederick, Maryland, and Haskall County, Oklahoma) hit the national headlines.

Finally, in 2005 the Supreme Court grasped the nettle in two cases, *McCreary County v. ACLU* and *Van Orden v. Perry*. The results were, to say the least, mixed. The *McCreary* case focused on the Commandments being displayed in two Kentucky courthouses. *Van Orden* dealt with a six-foot Commandments monument situated on the grounds of the Texas state capitol alongside other historical monuments.

In two rulings, both reached by close 5–4 decisions, the Court argued that the Texan display was acceptable (it had been there for 50 years, was surrounded by nonreligious monuments, and could be seen as serving a nonreligious purpose), but the Kentucky display was unconstitutional (it was inside the courthouses, and it *did* serve a religious purpose).

Needless to say, this pair of decisions caused great confusion, with advocates of competing opinions both having to swallow a defeat while celebrating a victory. The closeness of the Court's decisions, made possible by one justice, as it were, switching sides during the process, only added to the perplexity.

## PRESENT AND FUTURE TENSIONS

The Church–State war is currently being fought on a dazzling number of fronts. Take the issue of creationist teaching, for instance. Throughout the 20th century, various religious groups—almost always on the religious right—mounted a rearguard action against the dominance of evolutionary science. The famous Scopes monkey trial of 1925 was only the beginning of a long, often bitter contest in which advocates of creationism sought to have their message taught in the nation's public schools. The truth is, such ideas have never been far from the classroom in some parts of the United States, regardless of what the law says, but there have been many crucial moments in which the evolutionary–creationist tussle has entered the courtroom.

The issue of Church and State has been at the forefront of such proceedings. Creationists argue that they represent a reputable scientific alternative to the theories of Darwin et al. Their opponents suggest that creationism does not come close to being a legitimate scientific position. Rather, they argue, it is more like an article of religious, usually fundamentalist, faith. As such, it should not be taught as science in the classrooms of schools funded by the public purse.

The Supreme Court has occasionally dipped its toe into these waters. In 1968 it invalidated an Arkansas law that sought to ban the teaching of evolution, and in 1987, in the case of *Edwards v. Aguillard,* it attacked a Louisiana act that called for the equal treatment of evolutionary and creationist theories in the state's public schools. The act in question prohibited the teaching of evolution-science unless "creation-science" was also included in the curriculum. A group of citizens, including Don Aguillard, an assistant principal at one of the state's schools, claimed that this was unconstitutional. In his majority decision, Justice William Brennan ruled that the act failed to meet one of the standards of the Lemon test—that an act should have a valid secular purpose; rather, the act in question sought to undermine evolutionary theory by "balancing" it with creationism, which was, essentially, a religious teaching. The notion that the law was intended to secure academic freedom was adjudged a "sham."

This was a major blow for the creationists, but especially in the South, they did not give up the fight. In recent years they have adjusted their strategy and begun to talk about the notion of Intelligent Design (ID): the idea that, at some level, the wonders of nature can be sensibly explained only by reference to the handiwork of a supreme being. Many commentators have, with some justice, suggested that this is merely old-fashioned creationism in new clothes. They argue that ID scholars and institutions, most notably the Discovery Institute, are simply applying a veneer of scientific respectability to a religiously motivated enterprise.

Again, this is an argument that looks set to continue. In recent years there have been many showdowns over local school curricula, the use of ID texts, and the debates within some state legislatures about enacting laws that, on the spurious grounds of protecting academic freedom, might allow creationist ideas to enter the public school via, as it were, the back door. The 2005 case of *Kitzmiller v. Dover Area School District,* in which a federal district court in Pennsylvania averred that the teaching of ID in public schools was unconstitutional, garnered interest across the nation.

***

Many other controversial debates rumble on. There is the issue of legislative prayer, for instance. It had long been the habit of political institutions across the United States to open and close their sessions with a moment of prayer. In the 1983 case of *Marsh v. Chambers,* dealing with just such a practice in Nebraska, the Supreme Court decided, by 6–3, that it was not a violation of the establishment clause for either Congress or any state legislature to appoint and pay a chaplain who was charged with delivering prayers.

The Court opined that such a practice had the backing of tradition—such prayers were said in the very Congress that enacted the First Amendment itself and were sanctioned by two of the most devotedly separatist colonies in the early Republic, Rhode Island and Virginia. Hammering out the consequences of this decision has not always been easy, however, and there have been heated debates about what kinds of prayer are acceptable (sectarian as opposed to nonsectarian) and about how far the judgment in *Marsh* should extend—is it simply operative in legislatures, or does it also apply to, for instance, meetings of school boards or public courtrooms? Virginia, for instance, has recently been embroiled in a heated argument over the rectitude of police chaplains reciting sectarian prayers.

Similar bafflement has accompanied the question of the Pledge of Allegiance. Invented in the late 19th century, the pledge was voiced for several decades without any mention of religion. Then, in 1954, the phrase "under God" was added. Some Americans have seen this as a blatant assault on Church–State separation: living with tradition and historical precedent is one thing, but sanctioning innovation is quite another. In 2002 the atheist Michael Newdow won a spectacular victory in the U.S. Ninth Circuit Court of Appeals. The court agreed that it was wrong to force Newdow's children to recite the amended pledge: given the coercion involved (not to recite the pledge would have damaged the standing of the children), this was an "impermissible endorsement of religion."

This decision resulted in a frenzy of activity, and the old specter of prayer amendments once more raised its head. In 2004 Newdow was to be found in the Supreme Court, as plaintiff in the case of *Elk Grove Unified School District v. Newdow*. On this occasion, the Court rather dodged the issue, refusing to treat it as a First Amendment case on the technical grounds that Newdow was not entitled to bring suit on behalf of his child. Once again, this looks like a battle that is destined to rear its head again in the years to come.

***

Two other contentious topics have dominated the Church–State debate during the past decade. First, there is the issue of school vouchers. The divide between America's public and private schools is clear for all to see. However, there are occasions when the private and public spheres collide. We have seen this already in Supreme Court cases that dealt with public funds being spent on busing children to private schools, or public moneys being lavished on materials and personnel aimed at private school students. The school voucher issue is, in many ways, the continuation of this constitutional headache.

The 2002 case of *Zelman v. Simmons-Harris* asked whether such a voucher program in Ohio violated the establishment clause. The state-sponsored program offered scholarships to children, with preference given to low-income families. It allowed parents to send their children to private schools at reduced tuition fees. Crucially, 46 of the 56 participating schools had a religious orientation. Doris Simmons-Harris challenged the constitutionality of the scheme.

The decision of the Supreme Court was that the Ohio program was neutral, based on private choice, and as such did not violate the First Amendment. It did not, at root, favor religious over nonreligious schools; it simply allowed children from impoverished backgrounds to improve their educational opportunities without any reference to religion.

In his majority decision William Rehnquist argued "that the program was one of true private choice, with no evidence that the state deliberately skewed incentives toward religious schools." This "was sufficient for the program to survive scrutiny under the establishment Clause."

One of the consequences of the *Zelman* decision was that it helped to make decisions about voucher programs a matter for the individual states. In 2006 the Court flatly refused to hear the voucher-based case of *Anderson v. Durham School Department.* Subsequently, there have been many state-level debates, with various state judiciaries (Colorado in 2004, Maine and Florida in 2006, Arizona in 2009) striking down voucher programs. The year 2007 saw a statewide referendum on the issue in Utah (60 percent of the voters voted against a voucher program), and 2009 saw a heated argument over whether one of the pilot voucher schemes, in Washington, D.C., should be ditched or renewed after its initial five-year run.

The second bone of contention, chewed endlessly by politicians and commentators of various stripes, has been the emergence of faith-based initiatives. The issue at stake is whether it is legitimate for publicly raised funds to be given to religiously based charities. Is this simply good for the public good and evenhanded in terms of doling out money to charities, or is it offensive to the establishment clause?

There is a long history of interaction between government and charitable religious groups. As early as the 1890s, the Sisters of Charity were providing succor to the poor of Washington, D.C., and from the late 1940s, significant government funds were being provided to religiously affiliated hospitals. Similarly, homeless shelters and child care groups run by religious groups have historically received pubic funds.

In 1988 the Supreme Court tackled the case of *Bowen v. Kendrick.* This dealt with some of the consequences of the 1981 Adolescent Family Life Act, which was intended to discourage sexual activity among teenagers. Funds had been given to both religious and secular organizations, but the rectitude of this initiative was questioned by the American Jewish Congress. In a U.S. district court it was decided that providing funds to religious organizations to promote sexual abstinence represented a violation of the establishment clause. The Supreme Court did not concur, however, and applying the rubrics of the Lemon test, it saw no breach of Church–State separation. Granting religious organizations funds in this instance served a secular purpose; its main effect was not the advancing of religion, and no excessive entanglement between government and religion had resulted. It is crucial to note, however, that this was another very close ruling (5–4), and even those who upheld the constitutionality of groups receiving funds under the terms of the 1981 act offered warnings against the potential dangers inherent in public moneys being given to overtly sectarian groups.

Modern faith-based initiatives had their origins in the mid-1990s, when Senator John Ashcroft succeeded in passing his "charitable choice" initiatives in Congress. The argument was that there was nothing wrong with religious charitable groups securing federal funding, provided that safeguards, protecting civil rights and liberties, were put in place. This was an extension of the principle, expressed in the 1988 case of *Bowen v. Kendrick,* that authorized religiously-affiliated agencies to receive government aid, provided that such funds were not spent on the direct promotion of religion.

The devil, as ever, was in the details. During the Bush administration, faith-based initiatives grew from strength to strength. Bush had favored the idea during his Texas years, and he quickly made it one of the main planks of his Washington administration, establishing a White House Office of Faith Based and Community Initiatives in January 2001. Millions upon millions of dollars were doled out.

Interpretative problems arose, however, when the recipients unabashedly included religious instruction, devotion, and evangelism in their charitable efforts. Was this not a case of the state paying a religious group to spread its particular religious agenda? Also, if such groups continued to deploy an exclusivist hiring policy—only employing those of specific religious beliefs— was this not an instance of the state supporting discrimination?

This is perhaps the most controversial of all contemporary Church–State issues, and in the past few years, there have been tussles over Baptist children's homes in Kentucky proselytizing to charges in their care, a District of Columbia ministry for homeless men insisting that people attend services before securing a bed for the night, a marriage-education program that places biblical instruction at the heart of its ministrations, a Baptist outreach initiative that puts Bibles in its charitable handout bags along with food, and—perhaps most famously of all—a rehabilitation program in Iowa's prisons that served up religion along with its reforming efforts.

Even if we seek to avoid partisanship, the realm of faith-based initiatives perhaps allows us room to reach a solid conclusion. The principle of faith-based initiatives seems to have garnered a good deal of public support (it routinely scores high approval ratings in opinion polls), but it has sometimes been flagrantly abused. Various organizations have clearly used public funds to directly further their religious interests. This doesn't mean that charitable religious organizations should not receive such funds, but they are surely obliged to check their evangelism at the door. There is accommodation, and there is turning a blind eye. It is a huge pity that, so far, the Supreme Court has tended to steer clear of the issue (in 2007 the Court ruled in *Hein v. Freedom from Religion Foundation* that taxpayers are not entitled to challenge charitable-choice projects that have been initiated by the executive branch of the government).

## SUGGESTED READING

Summaries of important Supreme Court decisions can be found in John J. Patrick and Gerald P. Long, eds., *Constitutional Debates on Freedom of Religion* (Westport, CT, 1999); Robert S. Alley, ed., *The Constitution and Religion. Leading Supreme Court Cases on Church and State* (Amherst, NY, 1999). More general books about the history of Supreme Court activity in the realms of religious freedom and Church and State are Catharine Cookson, *Regulating Religion. The Courts and the Free Exercise Clause* (New York, 2001); Terry Eastland, *Religious Liberty in the Supreme Court* (Washington, D.C., 1993); Frank S. Ravitch, *Masters of Illusion: The Supreme Court and the Religion Clauses* (New York, 2007).

On the issues of evolution and creationism, see Michael Lienesch, *In the Beginning: Fundamentalism, the Scopes Trial and the Making of the Antievolution Movement* (Chapel Hill, NC, 2007); and on the recent case in Dover, Pennsylvania, see Edward Humes, *Monkey Girl: Evolution, Education, Religion, and the Battle for America's Soul* (New York, 2007).

On religion, education, and school prayer, see David Ackerman, ed., *Prayer and Religion in the Public Schools* (New York, 2001); Robert Alley, *Without a Prayer: Religious Expression in Public Schools* (Amherst, NY, 1996); Joan DelFattore, *The Fourth R: Conflicts over Religion in America's Public Schools* (New Haven, CT, 2004); Bruce Dierenfield, *The Battle over School Prayer: How Engel v. Vitale Changed America* (Lawrence, KS, 2007); Kent Greenawalt, *Does God Belong in the Public Schools?* (Princeton, NJ, 2005).

On the Jehovah's Witnesses, see David Manwaring, *Render unto Caesar: The Flag Salute Controversy* (Chicago, 1962); M. James Penton, *Apocalypse Delayed. The Story of the Jehovah's Witnesses* (Toronto, 1985); Shawn Francis Peters, *Judging Jehovah's Witnesses: Religious Persecution and the Dawn of the Rights Revolution* (Lawrence, KS, 2000).

See also Bruce T. Murray, *Religious Liberty in America: The First Amendment in Historical and Contemporary Perspective* (Amherst, MA, 2008); Randall Balmer, *God in the White House: How Faith Shaped the Presidency from John F. Kennedy to George W. Bush* (New York, 2008); Marvin Frankel, *Faith and Freedom: Religious Liberty in America* (New York, 1994); Isaac Kramnick and E. Laurence Moore, *The Godless Constitution: The Case against Religious Correctness* (New York, 1997); Frank Lambert, *Religion in American Politics: A Short History* (Princeton, NJ, 2008); Leonard Levy, *The Establishment Clause: Religion and the First Amendment* (New

York, 1986). And for a lively account of many contemporary controversies, see Peter Irons, *God on Trial: Dispatches from America's Religious Battlegrounds* (New York, 2007).

Though it ranges far beyond the American continent, a good place to begin searches for further reading on many of the subjects discussed here is James E. Wood Jr., *Church and State in Historical Perspective: A Critical Assessment and Annotated Bibliography* (Westport, CT, 2005).

# Afterword

The history of Church and State is much older than America, but one of that history's most dynamic chapters has unfolded there. For five centuries, discussions about Church and State have enraptured and puzzled the best of American minds. They have also drawn a crowd, and as a result, sophisticated theorizing has sometimes given way to demagoguery. There have been both wonderful highlights and moments for lament. The collision between the two forces us to abandon any idea that the United States offers robust solutions to a dilemma that has confounded the Western imagination ever since Constantine ascended to his throne in the fourth century.

Here, in 2010, the United States, for all its legal scholars, historians, and commentators, is still in a muddle when it comes to analyzing the proper relationship between faith and politics. The one thing it has in its favor, however, is a legal process. No one could doubt that this process is sometimes the plaything of shifting political and ideological currents. In recent years, this has become increasingly obvious. But for all that, there is at least the dream of a final standard, the hope of a binding adjudication. The rule of law, applicable to the entire citizenry, is still a concept to be conjured with, and given the alternatives, it measures up rather well.

Americans are always going to disagree about the relationship between Church and State, but although this can sometimes seem infuriating and confusing, it might just be a wonderful thing. Throughout this book we have seen how lofty legislative pronouncements have struggled to hold good in the confusion of changing historical circumstances and the workaday world of local American life. The most erudite scholars can't agree, and neither can school boards or state legislatures.

The battles will continue: about school prayer, about Christmas trees, about creationism, about which justices ought to sit on the Supreme Court's bench. Come election time, there will always be grumbles about religious groups, whose tax exemptions rely on some measure of studied political neutrality, endorsing political candidates.

In the past decade, old and new controversies have competed for the oxygen of publicity. Some have seemed vitally important: for example, the Christian right's campaign for a marriage amendment that inflicts its religious vision on the whole of the American republic and the squabbles over school vouchers and faith-based initiatives. Even during the final stages of this book's writing, old favorites reemerged: in Greece, New York, people argued about the rectitude of saying prayers ahead of school board meetings; in Missouri eyebrows were raised when Bibles were circulated in public schools; in Wisconsin the issue at hand was high school graduations taking place in a church; in Louisiana it was public funds being earmarked to send students to a Jesus Prayer Crusade; and before too long, we'll hear much more about a cross being displayed in California's Mojave national preserve.

Other issues can seem trivial. In the past couple of years, we have seen a case coming before a federal court tackling the issue of whether a branch of the U.S. Post Office ought to be set up in a Connecticut church. In South Carolina, people wondered if state-supplied license plates should be allowed to carry Christian messages. In New Jersey there was consternation when fire trucks ferried a statue of the Virgin Mary between churches.

In fact, such parochial controversies aren't trivial at all. They represent the front line of America's Church–State debate, and in their way, they are every bit as important as the manifestations of older, supposedly more newsworthy Church–State confrontations.

The debate continues. In some areas, workable solutions are well within reach. In others, they are as distant as ever. This makes legal decisions tortuously difficult, but it also makes for an endlessly fascinating historical narrative: one that shows no signs of running out of steam.

# Index

## About the Author

Dr. JONATHAN A. WRIGHT, who holds a doctorate in history from the University of Oxford, is an independent scholar who has published on many aspects of American and European religious history. He is the author of *Shapers of the Great Debate on the Freedom of Religion*; *God's Soldiers: Adventure, Intrigue, Politics, and Power*, a study of the Jesuit order; and *The Ambassadors: From Ancient Greece to the Nation-State*, a history of diplomacy. Dr. Wright currently is writing a history of Christian heresy.